THE OTHER MAN

21 WRITERS SPEAK CANDIDLY ABOUT SEX, LOVE, INFIDELITY, & MOVING ON

EDITED BY PAUL ALAN FAHEY

jms books

THE OTHER MAN

JMS Books LLC
10286 Staples Mill Road # 221
Glen Allen, VA 23060
www.jms-books.com

ISBN: 9781483970967

Printed in the United States of America

CONTENTS

Introduction 1

What If? by Jeffrey Ricker...5

The Rival with a Thousand Faces by Glen Retief..................... 15

The Hat Prize by Jason Schneiderman 25

Husbands by Austin Bunn.. 31

In the Brokenness of Summertime by R.W. Clinger 45

Any Resemblance to Actual Persons, Living or Dead, Is
Entirely Coincidental by Tom Mendicino................................... 57

Complicity by Mark Canavera 67

Turbulance by Chuck Willman.. 75

Just Wally and Me by Allen Mack... 83

Way Off by David Pratt 91

A Pitiless Love by Perry Brass.. 107

Where Are You Going To? by Paul Alan Fahey....................... 119

Thomas by Jeff Mann 125

Ballad Echoes by Erik Orrantia 137

The Other Side of the Game by Philip Dean Walker 147

Three's a Charm by Wes Hartley.. 161

Last Tango in Cambridge by Lewis DeSimone........................ 169

You Without Me by William Henderson..................................... 181

And Then There Was One by Rodney Ross 193

The Child by Felice Picano 207

A Brief History of the Divorce Party by Rob Byrnes 219

The Contributors.. 231

Acknowledgements 241

INTRODUCTION

HE'S A TRESPASSER, an interloper, the peckerwood who gets between you and your lover, partner or mate. The male equivalent of Cleopatra, Mae West, and Jessica Rabbit rolled into one threatening package. He's an accident waiting to happen: the skateboarder 'round the bend, the smiling barista with the extra hot mocha, or the computer geek eager to retool your mate's hard drive. He's a relationship gatecrasher, bound by no rules and with no sense of fair play. Who is he? He's *the other man*, and like Caesar, he comes, he sees, he conquers, and leaves behind something akin to a lingering, twenty-four hour flu or at worst, a really bad case of the Black Death.

If we're young, in our late twenties or early thirties, there's a glimmer of hope. We pick ourselves up and move on. If older, our new best friend might be our analyst or possibly the urologist we now see on a regular basis.

As the walking wounded, we don't eat. We can't sleep. We sense that the earth has stopped rotating. The minutes drag like hours, the days like years. We pass a mirror and see ourselves as we really are: unwanted and unloved. We are too fat, too short, too everything. We should have exercised more at the gym, lifted weights. Spent extra time on the treadmill, less in the Jacuzzi. We finger the dark circles under our eyes and notice the beginning of a double chin. Are those jowls? We notice wrinkles no sane person would ever call laugh lines. In desperation, we secretly check our partner's computer and search his emails. We open bedroom drawers digging for clues, evidence of his deception. We become other man detectives.

▲

ON THE FLIP side, *we* can be the other man, charging in and breaking the bonds of a committed relationship, sometimes without a thought to the pain and misery we inflict on the injured parties. Face it. We're not all innocent bystanders in other-man scenarios.

And sometimes we are guilty of nothing more than falling in love with the wrong person...or the right person at the wrong time.

In a committed relationship, open or monogamous, we can be tempted to stray, to crave something new: a different taste, a dude with a tighter body, or one with a sharper mind. Just as we covet a faster car, a smarter phone, a bigger bank account, or younger looks, we can be drawn magnetically to a string of horny husbands, to a one-night-stand, or to the guy lifting weights and strutting his stuff in front of us at the local gym.

In these true and riveting essays, twenty-one of our foremost writers dig deep to discover the truth about infidelity while tackling the subject with candor, courage, wit, and poignancy. They explore the contours, curves, and complexities of this seductive yet unpredictable creature from varying points of view, either by being the other man, suffering the other man, or by dealing with infidelity in their relationships. In a number of cases, writers state or imply that *other man* experiences have strengthened their unions and contributed to personal growth.

Glen Retief, in his early thirties and living in Spain with the man he believed was "the love of his life," experiences the ultimate betrayal when he confronts his lover's deception head on in "The Rival With a Thousand Faces."

Mark Canavera, while working for a large international organization in war torn Côte d'Ivoire (Ivory Coast), discovers that men, gay or straight in that culture, would never think of divulging an indiscretion to their partners. Telling would be viewed as an insult. In "Complicity," we discover, as expected, that other man troubles are indeed universal.

Perry Brass responds to an intriguing letter from a married—soon to be separated—fan in "A Pitiless Love" and finds himself sucked into an "emotional vacuum" that threatens his mental and physical health.

Erik Orrantia is in a committed relationship when he falls out of love with his partner. Unable to make a clean break, Erik invites his new lover to move in with the unhappy couple. Mr. Orrantia's essay, "Ballad Echoes," underscores the need for honesty in matters of the heart and suggests that triangles, of the human or two-dimensional kind, are better left to novels and the study of high school geometry.

David Pratt's partner juggles two other men on the side while pursuing his dream of becoming a professional actor in the Big Apple. In "Way Off," David offers us a personal tour of the Great White Way and points out the traps and pitfalls for those seeking fame and adulation in this world of dreams and brightly lit marquees. For David, the Broadway stage became a player in his relationship, a formidable opponent and the real other man.

In "Husbands," Austin Bunn looks back on his thirties in Louisville, Kentucky. Loneliness leads him to a succession of liaisons with married men: a chief researcher at a public health office, the boss of an automotive business, a lawyer, a pastor, and a professor at a Christian college. Somehow, there is always an abundant and available supply.

As most of these insightful essays convey, AIDS is still with us and still very much a threat after four decades, and it continues to be a major concern especially in matters of infidelity. Felice Picano's "The Child" and Chuck Willman's "Turbulence" offer moving portraits of men living and loving in the shadow of this devastating illness.

A casual encounter with a man in an adult bookstore that leads to a one-night stand inspires Tom Mendicino to write his first novel. It's no accident he titled his essay "Any Resemblance to Actual Persons, Living or Dead, is Entirely Coincidental."

R.W. Clinger devises an original, yet shocking, method to punish his lover's unfaithfulness in the essay, "In the Brokenness of Summertime," while William Henderson, married with two young children, struggles with his love for a "recovering" crystal meth addict.

Lewis De Simone, Jeff Mann, and Philip Dean Walker explore the enduring and wistful nature of first loves, lost loves, and the lure of the unobtainable. Jeffrey Ricker, Allen Mack, Jason Schneiderman, Rob Byrnes, and Wes Hartley offer a lighter approach, proving that, though painful at the time, humor is often the best cure for the other man dilemma—along with style, grace, and a little revenge.

Sometimes, if we're lucky, our relationships stand the test of time and actually last. While other unions dissolve around us, we become The Other Couple—a stable, unchanging presence in our friends' lives. As exemplars of perfect twosomes, we dole out pearls of wisdom. We provide aid, sustenance, and comfort to the walking wounded yet are always mindful of the tightrope we walk. As Rodney Ross tells us in "And Then There Was One," we cross that line of neutrality at our peril and suffer the consequences.

What we learn from these gifted authors is that we must take heart, that it does get better, and one day our luck is bound to change. We either survive the bumps and detours in our relationship and weather the storms, or we resolve to move on. Hopefully, along the way, we'll meet someone new and simpatico, maybe even our long awaited soul mate, and life is indeed good again. As it should be.

Paul Alan Fahey
Nipomo, California

WHAT IF?
JEFFREY RICKER

HAVE YOU EVER played *what if?* You know, where you take one moment or event in your life and ask, what if I'd done the exact opposite? What if I'd turned left instead of right? What would be different now?

The summer of 2003, I pretty deliberately started living out that game. I asked myself, *What if I were a big old slut?*

Maybe I should back up and set the scene for the train wreck that was the summer of 2003. In May of that year, my heart got a little stomped on. It wasn't really the other guy's fault; he wasn't looking where he was going, and I foolishly put my heart right in front of his feet. This was not the smartest thing to do, but ten years ago I was even more naive than I am now. And let's face it: the smart thing is not always the most exciting thing.

On its own, the heartbreak might not have been enough to send me into the spiral that soon occurred, but on top of that, I herniated a disc in my lower back that spring. This is why I have since sworn off yard work. (When I herniated the same disc again in 2011, I swore off spinning classes. Apparently, the safest thing to do is nothing.)

But wait, there's more. I might not have been so freaked out even then, if my doctor at the time hadn't screamed at me over the phone, "You need surgery! If you don't get it, you might wind up paralyzed!" After this, I made an appointment for a consult with a neurosurgeon, left my office, and sat in my car and cried for a while.

Did I mention he's now my former doctor?

So yes, I was a mess that summer. For months afterward, I couldn't go running, which was the one outlet that had kept me from going completely insane before that. Once I lost access to my endorphin rush, the one release valve that kept everything else from melting down was shut off. And boy, did I melt down. It got to the point where I wasn't able to do the basic things to function. Days went by where I barely ate. For a while, it seemed like I was living on Aleve and merlot. I got so skinny, co-workers told me the shape of my face was changing.

Who knew depression was the surefire way to reach my goal weight and beyond? And doesn't it sound like the perfect state of mind to think about dating?

Looking back, I see how ridiculous my reaction was to the situation. I was wallowing, and I knew it. The only thing that surprises me now is that I was at all surprised at the time. But that's the luxury of hindsight: You get to look back and realize what a complete idiot you were ten years ago, confident now in the fact that you'd never do anything so foolish as what you did back then.

I barely knew the guy who broke my heart, but that hadn't stopped me from jumping right into the deep end. Too bad the pool was empty. As I soon learned, though, when you wipe out in the deep end, there's still the shallow end to consider.

This was around the time when I also discovered that online dating sites, which I'd flirted with in the past, were also very useful for arranging booty calls. (Fine, call me slow on the uptake, but this was before smart phones, Grindr, Scruff, and whatever other mobile apps are littering the digital landscape these days. Now you can order up a piece of ass without even getting your own ass off the couch to turn on the computer. O brave new world that hath such wonders in it.)

Online dating was uncharted territory for me. While I wouldn't call myself a prude, up to that point I'd never given my friends much of a reason to think otherwise. I only started dating guys in my mid-twenties, never very frequently or for very long. (I told myself I was concentrating on my career. In hindsight I can only ask myself, *What career?*) All of my attempts at dating tended to fizzle out around the two-month mark. For the longest time, six weeks seemed like the hurdle I'd never get over. By the time the summer of 2003 came around, I'd say I started making up for lost time.

I can't say that I was very discerning in my selections that summer. I had only two criteria: Potential dates had to be within a fifteen-minute drive and be reasonably attractive. Both of those requirements were negotiable, though. I don't know why I thought dating in that state of mind was a good idea, but it didn't seem to be much of a hindrance. Apparently skinny and depressed were the qualities a lot of people found desirable.

Oh, who am I kidding? These guys didn't really care about my state of mind—at least, most of them didn't. Not that I cared much either. I had a feeling I was being foolish, but when your head says, "Are ya nuts?" your libido answers, "Yeah, baby!" and your heart says, "Leave me out of this; I'm on sabbatical."

Guess which one talks the loudest? The dumbest one, of course. That's how you end up getting it on with more guys in one summer than you have in your whole life up to that point—which still isn't all that high of a number. In hindsight (and maybe because the memory is the first thing to go), few of the guys I met that summer remain particularly memorable.

There were a couple exceptions.

First, there was the Ballcap Guy. I swear, I can't remember if he even took it off during sex. I also can't remember his name, either. Sad, I know, but I don't really remember many names from that summer. I recall them from details, like the built guy with the hairy chest and a beard—as in a girlfriend. The guy with the cat. The tall one who came over in the middle of a thunderstorm and then couldn't get it up—must have been afraid of lightning. There certainly wasn't any lightning inside my house that night.

But back to Ballcap Guy. I'm assuming there was a bald spot hidden underneath the hat, but I can't remember. Likewise, I can't remember what the arrangement was between him and his partner. Ballcap Guy never elaborated, except to say that their relationship was "way open."

I'd never encountered that phenomenon before, the open relationship. For some reason—let's hear it for naiveté—it had never occurred to me before then that such an arrangement was even possible, or that it could work. "Open relationship"—what did that even mean, anyway? Cheating without consequences? What were the ground rules? What did my participation make me? I suppose there are some people who can make that work, although I seriously doubt I'd ever be one of them. Does that make me a hypocrite?

There were a couple things that made carrying on with Ballcap Guy complicated for me. One, it turned out he and his partner were friends with a lesbian couple I knew. I really didn't want it getting around that I was, well, getting around. (Ten years after the fact, I guess I've found that it doesn't bother me as much as it used to.) At the time, I worried about them thinking less of me—and if I was worried about that, clearly I had some problems with what I was doing.

Not enough to stop doing it, mind you, but still.

The other problem with Ballcap Guy was his habit of keeping up a steady stream of dirty talk while we were having sex. A little of that goes a long way. A lot of that and I want to get out my red pen and start editing. "I'm sorry, what do you mean when you say you want me to fuck the cum out of you? Do you mean that you want me to fuck you until you cum? How long will that take, exactly? How long is too long? What if I'm done before you?"

I didn't say any of this out loud, of course.

The third problem wasn't really an issue with Ballcap Guy, but with me. Having a lower back issue often made sex a comedy of errors. My injury was healing, but I lived in fear of doing something that would make it even worse. So sex involved a lot of props and extra instructions, none of them the sexy kind: "Put this pillow under your back. How about if I lift your leg so...Okay, maybe if you move instead of me. Ow—no, not my back, my leg." Why they put up with this from me, I don't know. If nothing else, at least the situation offered me a preview of what sex will be like after I've qualified for AARP. Assuming I can still even have sex by that point.

Eventually, there was only so much of Ballcap Guy's dirty talk I could take, so I moved on. After him there was the one I'll call the Green Giant, because he was tall enough to make me (at six feet) feel short, and, well, I was a bit of a "ho ho ho" that summer. We made contact on the now-defunct Out in America—really, if those dating/pickup sites were honest in their marketing, they wouldn't say "Meet your next boyfriend" so much as "Meet the next guy you're going to shoo out of your house at three in the morning after you've had your way with him." In this case, I was the one being shooed. I remember the site I used the most often had checkboxes for what you were looking for—friends, dating, a relationship, or whatever I can get. If I remember right, I checked the last box. As I said, my standards were high.

The Green Giant sort of broke the curve though, because he was quite the catch. I'd seen him out and about before and had always found him attractive—tall, fair skin, a disarming smile. His boyfriend worked out of town most of the year, and while the cat's away...Well, I guess he and the mouse had an understanding. He sent me a message and we made plans to get together.

St. Louis is the biggest small town you'll ever encounter. The gay community is similarly compact. It makes it difficult to meet people who don't already know or have slept with half of your friends. Six degrees of separation is more like two, and when you think of all the people you've had sex with who've had sex with other people you know, it makes you want to take a *Silkwood* shower.

Because of this, it came as no surprise to me to discover that the Green Giant and I had friends in common. I found this out before he and I hooked up, when I went to a party at a friend's house and boom, there he was sitting in the living room. I didn't ask if the other nice-looking tall man with him was his partner. (As I discovered later, it was. Lucky guy, both of them.)

I did my best to stay on the other side of the room for the whole evening, though we did say hi eventually. I mean, what do you talk about in situations like that? "So nice to see you, and I'm really looking forward to seeing you naked when we have our booty call next week." Sadly, I don't think Miss Manners ever established guidelines for situations like that. I can just imagine: "When encountering a potential trick in an unrelated social situation where his boyfriend/husband/judgmental best friend is also in attendance, be polite, gracious, and express interest in his likes and dislikes. In mixed company, those likes should not include references to bondage, groups, or BDSM."

I guess it shouldn't have surprised me that eventually I would run into guys who wanted a little something on the side. According to statistics cited by the Kinsey Institute, between 20 and 25 percent of men engage in extramarital sex at least once during their marriage. Other studies put the number between 30 and 60 percent, which seems like too wide a spread (so to speak) to be statistically meaningful. And those are just the straight ones. Gay men? I know married couples who mess around more than some of my single friends. No matter how you look at it, there's a whole lotta home wrecking going on.

I certainly never expected to be a home wrecker myself, but that's another thing that surprised me: No homes were wrecked in the making of my summer of sin. Each time I got involved with someone in a relationship, it was without consequence— for the couples involved, at least. This threw me for a bit, especially the first time I came to the Green Giant's house. It wasn't a hustle-me-up-the-stairs-then-out-the-back-door thing. We had a drink, sat in his living room, and talked for a while. The house was comfortable, not too overly put together like a lot of gay men's houses. This one felt lived in—the vacation photos of the two of them around the living room added to that sense. So when we set down our glasses and made our way upstairs, it seemed a bit...surreal.

Situations like that can wind up being a three-way, even when the third person isn't there. At least, that's the way it was for me with the Green Giant. I couldn't put out of my mind for very long that there was another person in his life with whom he probably did the same things he did to and in and on me. In fact, there were a few other persons, since I wasn't the only one he was sleeping around with. And when his boyfriend was out of town for weeks at a time, he apparently did the same thing. I couldn't say his boyfriend was ever completely out of my mind except when we were having sex. The rest of the time I found it difficult to mentally multi-task.

When the Green Giant said he wanted friends with benefits, though, he really did mean friends. We talked about writing; he got me tickets to a show; he invited me to dinner with a group of friends of his. He even tried to fix me up with someone—of course, he said it would be nice if a three-way came out of that arrangement. (Neither scenario, the date or the three-way, came to pass.)

At some point, though, I realized I would have to stop carrying on like I was. "I'm sure this is going to get old after a while, this sex on a dime," I told my friend Lee, who was both the angel and the devil on my shoulders during that summer. He didn't see anything wrong with what I was doing with the Green Giant—he was even a little envious, since Lee had propositioned him at one point and been gently let down. As far as I could tell, I was the only one who saw anything wrong with what I was doing. But what was the problem, exactly? The

Green Giant was smart, charming, witty, cultured, well-read, well-hung, kind, and handsome. In short, he was everything you could want in a boyfriend.

That was the problem, of course.

I was having fun, I told Lee, but there's fun and then there's happiness. If you're sleeping with someone whose heart is already spoken for, you're not going to get much more than his dick or his ass—even when both of those are very nice, as they were in the case of the Green Giant, it's not enough. In the back of my mind, I was still stinging from getting my heart broken at the beginning of the summer and was trying to avoid dealing with it. The physical pain from my back injury just gave me an external sign of it. I was limping on the outside as well as the inside.

"Fuck the pain away," some of my friends told me. Well, they couldn't say I didn't try. Thing is, when you put your clothes back on and say good night, you're still there in your own skin, and nothing has changed except you probably need to take a shower when you get home.

When I left the Green Giant's home early one morning, I couldn't help but wonder, *If there are no lies involved, and no one is cheating, am I the only one involved who's deceiving himself?*

I wondered if I would be ready to give up the casual sex I'd been having a lot of during the summer if any of those men or someone else entirely became the focus of my interest. Clearly, though, that wasn't going to be the Green Giant. Finally, I told him I wanted to drop the benefits but still be friends. It turned out that worked just fine and was much less awkward than I expected it would be, even when I did finally meet and get to know his boyfriend—who's now his husband. So I can't say things didn't work out well in the end for them.

Eventually, I also stopped being a slut. Since running was out of the picture for a while, I took up swimming to get my endorphin fix. Doing laps in the pool was less of a logistical problem than sleeping around, and the exercise was good for my heart in more ways than one. I also started dating a guy that fall. It didn't last for very long, but after him, I met the guy I'm still with eight years later. And no, our relationship is not the least bit open. Clearly, I'm too selfish for that.

So maybe that summer I learned I wasn't as flexible as I thought I might be. (I'm speaking metaphorically, of course.) Even so, I learned that I could wade in the shallow end of the pool longer than I thought. But eventually you have to either head for the deep end or you have to get out, towel yourself off, and stick to dry land.

THE RIVAL WITH A THOUSAND FACES
GLEN RETIEF

INFIDELITY MAY BE the oldest narrative conflict. In the *Epic of Gilgamesh*, the hero enrages the goddess Ishtar by rejecting her marriage proposal, because he has heard how she cheats on her male lovers. In the Garden of Eden, Eve's attentions wander from Adam to the snake—a thinly disguised allegory for sexual dalliance—and as a result humans become mortal. You might say as a species we received the death penalty for our tendency to stray from our mates. But among all the stories I've read that address extramarital sex, the one that most deeply haunts me— the one I keep coming back to, because it speaks most closely to my own experience—is Graham Greene's postwar classic, *The End of the Affair*.

Sarah, the adulterous heroine, and Bendrix, the protagonist, make love in a London townhouse during the Blitz. A V2 rocket hits them. Bendrix is knocked out and looks as though he is dead, but comes to, unharmed. Soon after this, Sarah leaves Bendrix. Bendrix assumes she has gone back to her husband, but later he suspects her of having what we might call an Other Other Man, a rival's rival. Ultimately, though, he learns she made a deal with God. If God saved Bendrix's life in the V2 strike, Sarah would leave Bendrix and return to her childhood Catholicism. Her "illicit" afternoon trips are to pray and confess in a church. In effect, Bendrix's secret rival is God Himself—

almighty, omniscient, impossible to outmaneuver.

I count myself fortunate I have never found myself in romantic competition with any deities—with any Allahs, Krishnas, or Jesuses. I have never been dumped by a guilt-ridden Christian believing he had to choose between me and his Savior. It is true that my husband, Peterson Toscano, spent his youth in ex-gay programs, where he met and fell in love with men before abandoning them out of a belief that homosexuality was sinful. But that all happened years before I met him, and today he is out-and-proud. Neither have I had a lover desert me for a Tibetan Buddhist monastery journey or a Lourdes pilgrimage. But my most dramatic experience of a partner's infidelity—the one that will always, for me, define the essence of what it means to be cheated on—nevertheless had, it seems to me, something of a theological quality about it, as if I were up against not a man but a spiritual archetype.

At the time, 2002, I was thirty-two years old and living in Madrid, Spain, with Alejandro—a balding, kind, intelligent, thirty-three-year-old graphic designer, whom I then believed without question to be the love of my life. We'd met three years earlier, in a bar, while I was on the final leg of a backpacking trip before heading to Tallahassee to pursue a creative writing doctorate. After a gloriously romantic week of walks, coffee, flea markets, and museum-hopping, he saw me off at the bus station with a single red rose. Two years later, after visits, emails, phone calls, and one major failed attempt on his part to get a work permit in Tallahassee, I passed my doctoral exams, drew a dissertation writing scholarship, and packed my suitcase for Madrid, where I would write an apprentice novel while figuring out a way to remain with him.

At first, my new life was magnificent. Cheese, cured meats, and olives at the market; vermouths and tapas at sidewalk cafés of a summer evening…I thought I had arrived in a cobblestone paradise, where people laughed, wrote poems and music, drank wine, and knew how to enjoy themselves. Although Alejandro was still in the closet with his father, a retired physician, the family welcomed me to their Sunday feasts of shrimp, lamb, and *gazpacho*. Alejandro's mother, a buxom woman who wore floral dresses and smiled a lot, told me, "I'm so glad you're with my son." His father was politely welcoming. He looked at me hard with his pale blue eyes, quizzed me about politics and soccer, and corrected my verb conjugations. Alejandro and I traveled to his family holiday apartment on the Mediterranean coast, where we swam in turquoise coves smelling of lavender, and to green Celtic Asturias, where we drank cider poured from ceiling-height barrels.

It wasn't too long, though, before the practicalities began to catch up with us. My temporary student visa—I had enrolled in afternoon Spanish classes at a local university—gave me no right to work or stay long-term. I had thought that with a looming doctorate in English, I'd be able to find a school to sponsor me as a language teacher, but as I spent my afternoons submitting CV's, calling university departments and language academies, and dropping by to talk to neighborhood ESL shops, I soon learned my lack of a European passport would preclude me from most legal work. Finally, there was the question of accommodation. Alejandro's apartment belonged to his father—it had served as his consulting rooms. Like most young Spaniards, Alejandro did not earn a living wage. What would happen when the old doctor needed to sell this property? Was it even ethical for us to live there, under the pretense Alejandro was "helping out a foreign friend"?

Soon the days seemed empty. Alejandro left early to commute to a publishing house in an industrial satellite town an hour and a quarter away. He got home at six or seven in the evenings, exhausted, he said, not just from the work itself and from the traffic jams, but also from the homophobic mentality of his employers—right-wing, Catholic supporters of the patriarchal Opus Dei movement. Alone in an unfamiliar city, I struggled to structure my days. In the mornings, I headed to my computer, ostensibly to write my dissertation, but my novel scenes and sentences seemed clunky to me—contrived, ham-handed. My creative sessions spiraled into hours spent watching BBC news. In the afternoons, discouraged by my unsuccessful job hunt, I wiped down windows. I bought and made dinner, cleaned and folded laundry. I read novels. When I got bored with all this, I strolled around the nearby La Vaguada mall, looking at the pants, shoes, cellphones, ceramics vases, and vacations I could no longer afford. Before long, I was feeling depressed and tired most of the time, taking long *siestas*, which ended with me trying to estimate the numbers of identical flowers stuccoed on the bedroom ceiling.

On any of those days, the easiest thing in the world would have been to go cruising. A quick train ride, and I would have had the pick of fifteen active downtown bathhouses. With so many men still living with their parents, the public gay sex scene was livelier than any I'd encountered in an American city. I could have played in the bushes with the men who ogled each other in the Retido park. I could have invited a swarthy South American from Gaydar to kiss, fondle, and gallivant with me in my study in front of the dictionaries, the reference encyclopedias, and the computer with the abortive apprentice novel.

But every time Alejandro and I had discussed monogamy vs. polygamy, he had been adamant he could never cope with knowing I'd had sex with another man. For him, fidelity was the most important thing in a relationship—the essence of its beauty and sacredness: a litmus test of its health.

"It would be like tearing a piece out of my heart, *mi amor*," he said. As I recall, we were sitting at a park bench on the walk from our apartment to La Vaguada mall when he said this. Retirees bowled and played dominoes on the pebbly strip between the sidewalks. Crows cawed and pecked at litter and food crumbs. "I just couldn't do it. It feels—impossible."

I, on the other hand, found it easy to separate sex from love. Getting fellated in a sauna would have tempted me from

Alejandro as easily as cake putting me off food. But the last thing I wanted to do was hurt this sweet, lovely man, who hugged me so tight my heart melted. Who held my hand at foreign art films: Ray and Bergman, *The Hours* and *What Have I Done to Deserve This?* Who cried when he read me stories about teachers being killed in the Spanish Civil War. So it was fairly easy for me to simply put all thoughts of extramarital sex out of my mind, like avoiding avocado because it upset my stomach.

But my depression worsened. By December, in the chilly gloom of winter, I was waking in the early hours of the morning, trembling from anxiety. Bouts of nausea plagued me. I skipped meals, stopped cooking and cleaning. *Failed writer*, I said as I deleted whole chapters. *Crushing student loans. Ruined life.*

Although I wasn't yet ready to admit it, today I believe I was falling out of love. What once seemed like Alejandro's delicacy now struck me as weakness. Shy vulnerability had morphed into immature passivity.

"Menos mál porque estás aquí," he would sigh when he got home from work—things are less bad because you're here. His bosses had moved him onto a line of books attacking lesbian and gay equality. "Such *hijos de puta!"* But whenever I raised the question of his coming out on the job, or even just looking for another position, he shook his head.

"I've tried before," he predicted, gloomily. "How would we eat if they fired me?"

At family gatherings he waited until his father was distracted by the television, then he surreptitiously kissed me on the cheek, giggled quietly, and lowered his voice a tone or two to ask *Papá* about the football score.

"You hate soccer," I noted later, as we walked home. "I feel fifteen again, sneaking around behind the old folks."

But Alejandro insisted he couldn't be honest. "He's too old. He could have a heart attack or something."

I was beginning to figure out Alejandro had problems with truthfulness. But I still felt sure he'd be genuine with *me*, that the man who tenderly whispered I gave him a reason for living—*¡una razon para vivir, mi cariño!*—that this man was who he seemed.

A dark spring evening, in February or March. We were in the bedroom. I recall the beautiful rich brown earth tones of the counterpane beneath us, a design he'd made; he'd also hammered together the base of the bed, with large drawers for storage. I remember, of course, the painting on the wall opposite, an undergraduate nude he'd done as an art student. Painted abstractly, with quick, crude brush strokes, it showed a group of faceless male bodybuilders, their physiques radically fragmented. Exaggerated biceps popped off the canvas. Pectorals exploded upwards. It was as though they constituted a repeating, infinite fantasy of masculinity—later, it seemed an exquisitely appropriate backdrop.

Probably we got onto infidelity via finances. A couple of weeks earlier, we'd received some good news: A U.S. study abroad program wanted me to teach a class. If I was able to head home to Florida to pick up a visa, they would sponsor me for a yearlong work permit. No guarantees about the future, and the pay would barely cover my student loan payments, but still, I'd been looking for this all along—a way to stay. Alejandro and I were talking budgets and apartments, whether to stay in the family nest when I got back, or try to strike out independently, when Alejandro suddenly put his hand on my knee.

"There's something I need to tell you, baby," he said. "It's only fair you know before you do this." He caught my eye, and his voice cracked. "Oh, *mi vida*, you deserve this at least."

Does every Other Man talk worthy of the designation begin with a disclaimer? Looking back, I can't help feeling bitter. *Behavior*, I want to say to Alejandro. *Words are so extraordinarily cheap.* But in that moment, I simply stared at him, uncomprehending.

"What is it? What are you talking about?"

He sighed. "I have been having sex with other guys, *cariño*. At the bus station toilets, on the way home from work. Meeting them in their flats. I don't mean to. I don't want to. But I—I find I can't stop myself. It's been weighing on me, this secret. I don't want to lie to you anymore."

With hindsight, I notice the courage of this speech—the habitual closet-dweller coming out, unprompted. In the moment, though, I just feel up against a wall—that of my sheer naiveté. This cannot be true. I would have sensed something. A guilty, evasive look. A sated libido.

"Since when?" I ask. The words come out on autopilot. "How often?"

"Since…soon after you moved here. I tried, but—it became worse when you got—depressed."

"How often?"

He hesitates. His instinct is to hide again, but then he meets my eye and doesn't look away. He has promised himself, tonight, to come clean: He wants to leave behind falseness. "I don't know, baby. Most days, something, I suppose—during the week, I mean."

My stunned brain stirs. Something clicks: those very late evenings, with rose-turquoise summer light gathering on the balcony, as I heard the door latch turn. "*Mierda*, what horrible traffic."

"Have I hurt you, baby?" he asks now. "I'm so sorry, my love—I hate myself for doing this to you."

Yes, no question I'm wounded. Is this the core of it—feeling I have been living in a mirage? Shit, he said, when he got home—those awful buses—and a picture had formed of gridlocked highways, exhaust fumes, stale-smelling air-conditioning, the deafening growl of the bus engine. I'd felt for him, reached out and hugged him. But really, had there been—what?

Perhaps a suit-wearing Catholic boss, with a sweaty shirt. "Go home to that wife of yours, son." Alejandro had once admitted he displayed an anonymous woman to explain his wedding ring. "Good lad." Then, apparently a smooth ride back to the city, followed by an hour or two in a bus terminus bathroom. Secretive fumblings at the urinals. Sideways glances. A walk to a stranger's apartment—now, I masochistically can't stop myself picturing Alejandro bent over a kitchen table, with a middle-aged daddy patting him on the head. Back in our apartment, Alejandro collapsing in an armchair: "Ah, my love! Things are not as bad because you're here."

Yes—a blunt spoon scoops out my chest cavity. Yes—I want to punch this gentle, artistic man, start shouting and throwing plates around like an Almodóvar character: *You did WHAT?* But mixed in with this pain, pure intellectual curiosity also pricks.

"But you were the one who said you wanted to be monogamous! I offered openness. *You* were the one who said outside sex would be desecration. What's going on in that head of yours?"

"I know," he says, looking down now. "I still feel that way—about monogamy. Only—something stops me from being able to do it."

This is one definition of both the divine and the diabolical: something larger than ourselves. Talking to Alejandro that night, I began to feel up against an invincible competitor, a rival with a thousand faces, arms, legs, and penises—a contender who, by virtue of his expansiveness, would always be able to offer more variety than I could.

"Do you think we should open our relationship now?" In hindsight, my words seem so mealy-mouthed. Today, I wish I'd stood up for myself: *You've blown your chance, Alejandro. That's hardly the only thing you've blown, it seems, but it's the one that matters. From now on cruising is fine for both of us.*

But I wasn't ready yet for this confrontation, and who knows? Perhaps I was still in denial, believing he could change. Perhaps I was already plotting this as an exit strategy.

"Oh no, never! I really don't want do that, Glen." We ended up repeating this conversation several times over the next two months. Over and over again, I asked Alejandro how he was doing with monogamy, and he confessed, "I've slipped." Three, four, or five times, I suggested an open relationship, and he replied, "No, if you had sex with someone else, that would be the end for me. *Terminado.* I couldn't cope."

In Greene's *The End of the Affair*, Bendrix yearns for Sarah's love. But for Sarah, the proof of her commitment to Bendrix is her ability to keep her promise to God to *not* love him. So the more Bendrix wins Sarah's adoration, the more he loses it. Paradox. Checkmate. Defeat.

Similarly, for Alejandro the proof of our relationship lay in its exclusiveness. Not just on my part—Alejandro was too savvy to buy into a gay male version of the sexist double standard. No, the proof of how much he loved me—of how lovable I was to him—lay in how faithful he was able to be to me. And on that ground, I let him down without being able to help myself.

In the end, it became too much for me, his lack of self-control and closetedness on top of the relocation difficulties. "I can't be what you need," I told him at last, on the phone from Florida, explaining why I'd written to the Madrid study abroad director and told him I wouldn't be taking up his offer. "I can't unlock the magic box in your head. I can't unknot the contradictions."

"I don't understand them either," he admitted. "But you are everything to me," he added. "Everything, darling. The world." At that moment, I imagined a whole planet opening up. Oceans and continents, cultures and languages—the weekend we drove to Portugal and stood on the ramparts of a castle overlooking the majestic coastal plane. It all seemed too big a vista to attach to a single love affair, like trying to load a Pyrenee into a wheelbarrow, or attempting to lift a house-sized boulder with a pair of bare hands.

THE HAT PRIZE
JASON SCHNEIDERMAN

I WAS SO excited for our second date that I bought a new sweater. It was a really cute sweater. I was late to meet Michael because I was buying that sweater. But unlike our first date, the chemistry seemed wrong from the moment I arrived. The restaurant was a Greek restaurant. I always forget that I don't really like Greek food. When we sat down, my Prince Charming announced that he was about to take a Valium. I thought: *Couldn't you just tell me you're taking an Advil? Valium?* I watched a filmstrip in fifth grade about the dangers of Valium. You can't even kill yourself with Valium. Addictive, retro, lame.

The night I met Michael, we talked all night. On our first date, we talked so long the maitre d' had to let us know that the restaurant was closing. But now I was searching a menu for the least offensive option while the man across from me took a drug popular among 1950's housewives. Our conversation couldn't find a groove. I'd told my friends about him, which I figured was the jinx. I'd ruined it.

I'd been playing hard to get. My friend had just read *The Rules* (remember that book?), and I was no longer falling into bed on first dates. On our first date, he'd walked me to my door, but I didn't invite him up. I walked him to the subway instead. I thought it had been a good move, but now I was doubting myself. I should have gotten laid and been done with it.

Things were going so badly that I was on the verge of excusing myself and just walking out of the restaurant. I was trying to formulate the words in my head. *Sorry, this just isn't working?* Too vague. Too formulaic. *Look, I'm just not feeling the connection I did last Friday?* Also unworkable. And what would I do if I left? I didn't want to leave. I just wanted him to be the guy I remembered.

He ordered an appetizer, and then he broke the awkward silence. "I should probably tell you I have a boyfriend."

A boyfriend?

Seriously?

What's the line from *Party Girl?* Ah, yes. *You lower my real estate.* I'd just gone through this—though technically, I had been the boyfriend. I had spent my study abroad year dating a man named Alexei. He had cheated on me with roughly half the men in St. Petersburg. I had been completely duped, and it had been humiliating.

Well, at least I no longer had to excuse myself. "A boyfriend?" I said. He sheepishly nodded. "Have I been unclear?" I asked him. "Have I somehow sent you mixed messages? Were you not under the impression that this was a date?" I could feel the Joan Crawford in me rising. I was sitting up straighter, speaking with a level of disdain that I usually reserve for the what-I-should-have-said-but-would-never-be-so-bold-as-to-actually-say aftergame. I unleashed all the vitriol I had. When I finished, I sat back, self-righteous and wounded.

"You're being so nice about this," he said.

Nice? I was doing my best to be a total bitch about this.

"What's his name?" I asked.

"Fernan." He said.

"Is Fernan a name? Shouldn't it be Fernan*do*?"

He laughed. "It's actually Fernan Fernandez."

I laughed too. How could I not? I figured that the evening shouldn't be a total waste. "Can I still have sex with you?" I asked. To be honest, I wanted to see his apartment as much I wanted to have sex. I really liked seeing people's apartments.

"I was hoping you would ask that," he replied.

▲

HE HAD THE best apartment I'd ever seen. It was a two-bedroom off Columbus Circle in the building where Bela Bartok had died. The sex was fantastic. His taste in bedding was exquisite. His bedroom was cozy and perfect. I wanted to stay in his bed forever. My apartment had a bathtub that filled up with raw sewage and had to be bailed into the toilet. I had been showering at the gym for weeks. His bathroom, with its white porcelain tub and sliding glass doors, was heaven.

As I came out of the shower the next morning, he was on the phone with Fernan Fernandez. Michael was telling him about me. Or rather, he mentioned my existence, and listed my qualities. It was as odd as it sounds.

As I listened to them talk, I realized that they weren't talking. They were just recounting events. I thought to myself, why don't you two just exchange calendars and get it over with? But now that Michael was taken, and there was no risk of actually having to fall in love with him, we went back to the easiness of our first date. For the first time in my life, I wasn't auditioning a man for life partnership. For the first time in my life, I fell in love.

It happened gradually. Michael and I would often spend two or three nights a week together. Sometimes I'd spend the evening at his place, and sometimes he'd come to my place. He would leave my apartment at six A.M. to get back to his place to shower and change and be at work by nine A.M., which I found consistently impressive. Michael seemed to find all of my faults endearing. I am an incredible klutz, and Michael never minded when I spilled coffee—which I did every single morning we were together. I had a habit of basically living in my bed, and even after Michael was poked by the sharp end of a compass (I'd been drawing circles) while trying to sleep, he never objected.

We never seemed to stop talking. Once when we were

walking around Central Park with our Sunday morning coffees, I made some sententious statement or other and Michael asked me who had said that. "I did," I said, slightly annoyed. "If I'm giving you someone else's idea, I'll tell you. If it's not footnoted, it's mine." I was in my first year of grad school; I was belligerent and insecure.

Michael responded, "You're the first guy that's ever been smart enough for me." I was a little insulted.

"Have you been dating morons?" I asked. (Twelve years later, I've met many of Michael's exes. There is one whom I'm quite fond of, but for the most part I can confirm: Yes, he'd been dating morons.)

Michael also seemed to enjoy my mean streak. Once when we were discussing writing, he explained that for him writing poetry was a personal project. He told me that it was about self-expression and personal growth. I looked at him incredulously. "That's," I said, "what bad writers say when they can't get published."

Inexplicably, he found this endearing.

▲

I KEPT THE subject of Fernan off limits. Michael's roommate had developed a strong dislike of Fernan, and Michael often wanted to defend Fernan to me against the accusations of his roommate. Channeling Jeanne Tripplehorn in *Sliding Doors*, I had to point out that I was trying to be his boyfriend. "I'm not impartial here," I would say, "You talk about him to someone else."

Still, despite our growing affection, and increasing time together, there were times when Fernan would visit and I would have to disappear. I would meekly retreat to my post-apocalyptic apartment with its bad plumbing, aggressive rodents, and eviction threats. I would spend the time waiting for my life to restart when Michael would put his real boyfriend on a plane back to San Juan.

If I'd been following my own plan, those weekends without Michael would have been my most active husband hunting time. I'd explained my plan to Michael: Until Fernan was living in New York full-time, Michael was my pretend boyfriend. Since it's a proven fact that people in a relationship are always more appealing to single people, I would be using the extra attraction boost from having a pretend boyfriend to attract a real boyfriend. But of course, I spent most of our time apart wondering when I could see him again.

During one of the blackout weekends, I was having lunch with a friend when my jaw locked up. I was explaining my plan and suddenly I experienced intense pain in my jaw and I could barely move it. Clearly, my body knew how ridiculous the plan was, even if I didn't. Thank God for chiropractors.

▲

OVER TIME, MICHAEL and Fernan's relationship went into an irrevocable downward spiral, and it suddenly seemed like he wanted to complain to me about Fernan all the time. Again, I had to insist that I was not an impartial observer—I had a vested interest. I wanted Michael, but only if I could get him free and clear.

I began to insist on two points: 1) If you break up with Fernan, you do it because you don't want to be with him, not because you want to be with me. 2) I'm not plan B. Don't think that breaking up makes us instant boyfriends.

Michael wrestled with his feelings. It was almost impossible *not* to talk his relationship through. We discussed almost everything, and this one piece of our lives—perhaps the most consequential piece of our lives—was under conversational quarantine.

▲

THE NIGHT THAT Michael called me to tell me that he had broken it off with his boyfriend, he said all the right things. It was as though I had coached him. And of course, I had.

"It's over," he said, "and I know that doesn't mean that you're my boyfriend. I didn't break up with him to be with you—I did it because he wasn't right for me."

I cut him off. "We have to go to a Kentucky Derby party tonight. What do you have that we can put on your head? There are prizes for hats."

"I have a double-headed dildo," he replied.

"Awesome," I said. "Bring it. We'll run them through a pair of my briefs, and you can wear that for a hat."

We met up, and as we waited for the subway to Brooklyn, I wondered how long I would have to keep up this back-to-square-one charade. I'd been so focused on being certain that I had him free and clear, I wasn't sure how to actually have him. He looked down the track, waiting for the light, and holding a brown paper bag containing the illicit makings of his hat.

"You're my boyfriend," I said. I just blurted it out.

"What?" he said.

"You're my boyfriend," I repeated. "I know I said we'd have to wait and all, but you are. You just are."

"Okay," he said.

He won the hat prize by a landslide.

HUSBANDS
AUSTIN BUNN

"All actual life is encounter."
—*Martin Buber*

THIS IS HOW I find Daniel in my memory: naked, in my closet, on the phone with his wife.

"Are you in a tunnel?" I heard her ask. "You sound strange."

"I'm driving with the windows up," Daniel said. "Love you." He flung the phone onto the pile of his clothing and slid next to me on the bed, his eyes closed, an over-eager smile warming his face.

Daniel's photograph, the one he emailed yesterday, showed him wearing a bad tie and seated in an office chair, the ghostly slap of a computer spreadsheet paling his face. He claimed to be a photographer, for God's sake. Yet the total inhibition of his picture, the complete lack of self-awareness, was somehow the attraction. Or challenge. Or maybe this was charity. I still don't know. Here was a man who couldn't see himself. At least he laughed easily. When he did, he barked upwards, revealing a top row of teeth that came to a point, like the prow of a boat.

Initially, Daniel proposed I visit him at his office building during his lunch hour. This was to be my first encounter in a new city, and the thought of sex on industrial carpeting depressed the hell out of me. Driving to him, anyway, was out of the question. So I invited him over after work. An *amuse bouche*,

I called him. An appetizer. He didn't get the joke.

He was slim and shorter than me, with tremendously bushy eyebrows. A pelt of black hair covered his body, which I saw as some certification of masculinity, however imaginary. On his Manhunt profile, he said he had "suckable" balls—a straight man's idea of a gay man's idea of sexy. I felt like I was providing material to Daniel, fuel for his fantasy life, which I couldn't help but think, judging by his greediness, occupied increasing real estate in his actual life.

He emailed the following morning, "WOW! Sure would like to get invited back." He won't. I expected to date single gay men, not sleep with husbands. Months later, he found me online. He said he was unemployed, home and horny. I wished him luck with the job search. Hey, at least I wrote him. A month later, I received another note. "This is my final email to you. I am deleting the others."

Nine months later, I was standing in line at the airport security checkpoint and I spotted him, six people back. I waved and smiled without noticing his wife, dressed in a light-blue 1980's power suit, standing beside him. He looked away and she stared bluntly. Could she suspect nothing? I was in the realm of impossibilities.

The line was long, and for the next twenty minutes, Daniel and I snaked back and forth in the queue, passing each other by inches. I could have leaned over the rope and shattered his world. I was a cold, dangerous fact rising to surface and sinking again. As we shuffled along, I realized that, in the months I'd lived in Kentucky, I'd become the other man for more husbands than I cared to think about. I wanted Daniel to be the last married man I slept with, but he was only my first. I considered waiting for him on the other side of security, even though I had nothing to say. I wanted to prove that I was a nice person, that we shared an afternoon and that nothing washes off. But of course, I terrified Daniel and by some transference of doom, that really worried me.

▲

AFTER SIX YEARS living with my boyfriend, I accepted a fellow-ship in Louisville to write and teach while he headed to graduate school in Texas. Though I still cared for him, I didn't want a long-distance relationship, didn't want to pine or pretend that I would be faithful. So I moved to Kentucky a single man. "My leap year," I thought to myself.

I met my first husband the first week. For exercise, I ran the loop in Cherokee Park, the city's rolling, verdant sanctuary, and one morning, I got cruised by a walker, a man with a blustery Teddy Roosevelt stride and a gold wedding band. In the humidity, his damp T-shirt stuck to his chest. It looked like a breastplate of armor. We sat on a bench and he told me he'd been married for twenty years and owned a horse—his daughter's actually. It was the kind of topic you land on when you're in free-fall. "I've never been with a man before," he said. I put my hand, slick with sweat, on his impressive thigh. "Not here," he said, "I know too many parents."

I gave him my telephone number. "Tomorrow," I said.

"Tomorrow," he said.

The next day, when he didn't show, I was naive enough to think that he was sick or busy. For weeks, I looked for him, moving through irritation, bewilderment, and finally, a sense that I had come on too strong, that I needed to recalibrate my game for spookable Southerners or Midwesterners or wherever I was exactly. I gave up, stopped running and started yoga.

I learned quickly that my new bachelorhood came with a sharp loneliness. Soon, I circuited the city's five gay bars, shopping for a place to feel at home. Louisville is a major regional city, the largest in the state, and a catchment area for gay men. Though two of the bars were nearly empty, the third, The Connection, was a gigantic nightclub complex with multiple themed bars and hourly drag shows playing to packed houses. I found myself most at home at Tryangles, a wood-paneled pub with an interior porch, pool tables, and music low enough for conversation. I found that Louisville was, without a doubt, a stylish, gay-friendly city. I could live here. You could too.

But I noticed that the majority of the men at the bars and clubs in town were either much younger or much older than me. At thirty-four, I felt like a category of gay men was, for the most part, missing: professionals from their mid-twenties to forties. I suspected that, as with other areas of the South (and regional cities everywhere), gay men with ambition were trying out the big city. They sowed their wild oats in Chicago or Atlanta or D.C. They came to Louisville for college and returned when they wanted to buy a house and settle. That gave the city a sense of continuity and warmth; many people you met were *from* here, which you couldn't say about Los Angeles or New York. (In the four largest American cities, four out of five men who have sex with men are not from there, according to a 2006 study in the *Journal of Homosexuality*. And I'd spent my twenties in New York as one of these men.) This also meant that the available men that *stayed* in Louisville fit four types: men newly out of the closet (one guy I knew had just finally exited his second marriage), travelers driving through, terrible spellers I couldn't abide, and non-strivers who never wanted to leave. This may have been a harsh assessment and there were certainly exceptions. But this had been my experience. So of the stable, articulate, self-respecting men of my type, a good number turned out to be married. Nine months after my arrival, I had met and "known" more married men than gay men: a chief researcher at the public health office, the boss of an automotive business, a lawyer, a pastor, and a professor at a Christian college.

I was also late to the lessons everyone else had learned about meeting men, especially online. The word "discretion" was code for married. ALL CAPS or having no picture meant married or technologically medieval. And truthfully, if I discovered someone was married, I didn't write him off. Every gay person had a closet and some were more spacious. Besides, in my experience in Kentucky, the percentage of husbands who read books and knew that "What u up to?" wasn't an opener, far, *far* exceeded gay men. Husbands learned seduction theory. Their wives made them.

Many husbands had even cracked gay code. It was hard to distinguish one well-adjusted gay man from a husband on the down low. Husbands called themselves "bears," "daddies," or "uncut" tops, never "husbands." They knew the triggers, the lingo, their niche in the market.

In November, I met one husband for a drink. His profile headline read: *Athletic-Professional-Masculine—Hairy-8.5 Man Meat Clean Cut.*

I didn't know he was married, but "man meat" should have given it away. He described himself as "6'1, 210, 8.5LC, TOP, 46C, 35W," which didn't quite reflect the hyper man in flip-flops I met in person. Flip-flops are not really a first-date option. He wanted badly to be liked, even after I made it clear I wasn't feeling it. When I got home, I emailed him to wish him luck. The email bounced and his profile had already vanished. A week later, it reappeared. In lower-case.

Soon enough, I was spending a lot of energy on husbands. When I lived in New York, I don't think I'd met a one. What was it about me, or them, or here that brought us together? Many of my friends openly wondered what I was doing or what I saw in them. I started to ask myself, What was it doing to me?

▲

MARRIED MEN WERE prompt. They arrived at noon, in the morning, or at happy hour dressed in white sneakers with Velcro straps. Or in loafers with tassels. Their belts were cinched tight, as if they were trying to teach their bodies a lesson about who was in control. I had a rule that I didn't sleep with men who wore all-white sneakers. I had a rule. There were simply too many white sneakers out there.

Married men did not want a drink. Alcohol on the breath

would get noticed. They accepted a glass of water. They were uncertain where they belonged, whether or not they should go straight to the bedroom. They were happy to talk about their wives, partly, I thought, because their wives were the reason they were here. "She's stopped having sex with me since she went on her medication for depression," one husband said. "That was four years ago. I tried being good for a year, but that didn't work." Another said, "We still have sex but she has never done anything but lay there, and she would never do anything more."

Married men arrived empty-handed. They knew about condoms but they couldn't keep any. Whatever gear they might have had, mouthwash, Viagra, towels, they stashed in a gym bag at the office. They sat on the couch with their water and wiped their brows. It was my understanding that they had come to me because they were tired of initiating. In their everyday lives, the responsibility for sex fell almost entirely on them and they were exhausted. Married men wanted to be instructed. Widened. Surprised.

Even when no one had a view in, they wanted the blinds down because they didn't want to see out. It was easier to make this time exempt from the world that way. They really didn't see a problem with wearing socks and nothing else. They hung their button-down shirts on the doorknob and folded their pants. Wrinkles might get noticed. They left their watches on. They couldn't lose track.

What came next tended to be fast and directed. They might never have another chance. They wanted to kiss, more out of routine than desire, but I didn't. I had a rule about kissing. The *Pretty Woman* rule but it is still a rule. Surprisingly, they took instruction well, considering how poorly I suspected they took it elsewhere. They were collecting experiences, vistas to fire their inner life. They shed their inhibitions in the car ride over.

Afterwards, they sighed when they looked at their watches. They hardly ever showered. The smell of strange soap would get noticed. Their belts tightened again, shirts tucked back in, they jingled the coins in their pockets, raised the ringer volume on their phones. An hour later, I received an appreciative email asking for an invite back. Or I never heard from them again. Almost all I saw again online, looking. And I felt like they were a country I visited for an afternoon, hit the highlights, and took the first flight out.

The appeal of husbands came to this: convenience. Same day delivery was always free. There was no clutter, psychological or otherwise. In the economics of encounter, sex with gay men meant you might have to dress.

And husbands did not judge. For me, low self-esteem and frustration triggered the impulse to cruise. With husbands, I was easily beautiful. This worked both ways. My attention rewarded them, reassured them of their sexual viability. And this power to stoke a stranger's erotic life came with little emotional cost. Unlike younger women who might long for their time, commitment, or for an annulment, I was not interested in their happiness, nor was I burdened by expectations of further intimacy. These unavailable men did not test my commitment to my boyfriend—or was it my ex—1,000 miles away.

The encounters, while rarely better than good enough, almost always had the heat of genuine transgression. So much was new, so much of their bodies remained a mystery. Gay men who "do" casual sex, partnered or otherwise, were regulars at it. Their boundaries were more like theatre curtains than actual thresholds. They'd done before everything they'd do with you. But with husbands, their rote sense of pleasure was desperate for expansion. These affairs with other men created a dissonance in their sex lives: what they got at home and what was possible. "Your body is asking questions," I said to Paul, a married computer programmer. It was a line, I knew, but it worked.

Paul said, "Answer them."

⅄

I WANTED TO think these husbands lived on the blade of their contradictions, between behavior and identity, but how sharp was that edge? One husband finished, got up from his knees, and said, "I've been told that I'm good at that." Another husband, a dragon tattoo snaking up from his calf to his neck, told me that Satan made him seek out sex with men, and then asked for directions to the YMCA showers. Another spent six months at Dry Ridge, KY at an in-patient Pure Life Ministries counseling center. *Sotto voce*, he said he wanted to follow me into the bathroom at the coffee shop. I told him no. For an hour, I listened to the disaster of his life: the son-in-law who threatened to kill him for sleeping with men, his dishonorable discharge from the military. Why did I listen? Because he'd come a long way to this very moment. Because I was sitting across from a man with a haywire ego and it was interesting, like watching the demolition of a building.

We live in a compartmentalized era and sex with men, for husbands, was yet another drawer to manage. Diligently, they cleared the web histories. Inevitably, they called from the car. The Internet and cell phones have created more privacy, not less, these slim channels of desire. Still, married life and secret gay sex had to generate some anxiety, distress, and depression; in fact, distress and depression are more common in men who have sex with men—a category distinct from "gay" or "straight"—than men in general. (Seventeen percent more, says the *American Journal of Psychiatry*.) There are, no doubt, countless reasons for that, but the risks of a double life surely account for some. The social scientist Leon Festinger called this state of internal conflict "cognitive dissonance," when people experience two competing thoughts, like heterosexual self-image and homosexual desire, they seek coherence by resisting what they don't want to think about. In other words, denial.

But cognitive dissonance also creates *arousal*. Internal conflict is itself a turn-on. We know this intuitively. There's a reason why the possibility of gay sex with straight (or straight-looking or "straight-acting") men is such a common attraction.

The contradiction—the military uniform, the wedding ring—has a psychological power we have no control over. For some, it becomes a fixation.

The husband I met for coffee, the one with the disintegrating ego, emailed that he'd sought out men in adult bookstores for two hours after we met. Finally, he met a willing party. He wrote, *He had a wedding band on. ;)*

▲

IN FEBRUARY, I had a strange, almost ghostly experience. I can't explain it any other way except to say that in the middle of a drink with one of these husbands, I had the acute sense that I was talking to my father.

My parents divorced when I was four, precipitated by many factors but involving, most specifically, my father's infidelities with men. It's not a subject that my family talks about openly—my mother only confessed it to me on the car ride home from my freshman year of college—and my father is now remarried. He has never explained himself, and I'm not sure he could even if I wanted him to. At this point, years of shadows have settled into a simple dark. But with this talkative, thoughtful husband, who had three sons, I suddenly had the sense that I was approaching an old, very personal mystery. The German novelist W.G. Sebald says that we have "appointments to keep in the past," as if all the moments of our lives occupy the same space and "future events existed and were only waiting for us to find out a way to them at last."

This was my appointment, my chance to get a response from the decades past. By the end of that single beer, I understood that I had been wrong before. My *own* body was also asking questions. Why do these men do what they do? Could I give them, wholly, what they were looking for? Perhaps I was after a missing interaction with these husbands, an answer in skin. They wanted to feel, briefly, how their lives might be otherwise.

I wanted to know why it had been so.

▲

WHEN I THINK about my history with husbands, I have to think of my first. It's been ten years now, and Hal was an unlikely choice for an inaugural boyfriend. I was twenty-four; he was in his fifties, married with three kids. The last time I saw him, in Brooklyn's Prospect Park, he told me that he'd had a heart attack.

It was a warm September afternoon, and we sat together on a bench, overlooking the rolling main field. He was dressed, as he so often was, in shorts, a short-sleeve Hawaiian shirt, and sandals like he'd just come from a bonfire. I remember he had nice feet, considering the subways.

At one point in our six-month relationship, Hal promised to leave his wife for me, for this young man he'd met at the YMCA on 63rd Street. I know, I know. Hal wrote children's theatre and played the piano. I worked on Columbus Circle, for *Newsweek*, doing something indistinct with Prodigy and AOL that involved me writing many captions. We were both unaware of the cliché we were enacting at the YMCA, drawn to each other while surrounded by gay men, who watched this ancient drama unfold in front of them, pure theatre for its best audience. I'd never been with a man I'd found so beautiful and gentle, and yet pure burl. He had never been with a man before, except for an accidental hand-job in a rumble seat as a teenager.

We saw each other every weekend for half a year. He came to my place in Little Italy to lie in the hammock I'd strung up in my living room. He was immensely furred, to the point where, when he came out of the apartment shower, jury-rigged next to the kitchen sink, he looked like a drenched animal.

What did I get from Hal, or he from me? I think I was trying to coach Hal out of his passivity, to make him reach for me, for a man. He was teachable and safe. Often, he lay immobile in my bed, anticipating my expeditions. I never expected our relationship to last. Honestly, I don't know that he saw much of anything specific in me except someone who saw possibility and beauty in him. When he looked at me with desire, it looked to me like shyness.

Eventually, I decided to leave New York, to live in France and see who I'd become. The news destroyed him. He sat, frowning, on the modular, hand-me-down couch in my apartment. I had betrayed some unknown commitment he'd made in his fantasy life. My journal entry about this "final day" together is strangely cold, which I recognized even at the time. "I have never felt the anguish of heartbreak," I wrote then, though I have since. "Am I incapable? Or somehow blessed into always operating as the 'beloved?' And therefore immune?" The entry then concluded with some half-baked musings on *How We Die*, a book about the science of mortality. What could be colder?

That afternoon, years later in the park, I was glad to see him and he approached me with the same calming sweetness I'd loved before. I took him back to my apartment and asked to see his scar. A raised keloid seam ran from his belly to the sternum, where they had cracked his rib cage open. The pasture of gray-black hair on his chest had been shaved but was growing back. I was reassured to know that his body was reclaiming his surface.

A couple of years ago, I came across Hal's email address. Even more years had passed since we'd communicated and I decided to write him. I was curious about his well-being and his convalescence. I wrote, "When I look back and wonder when I knew I was gay, I think of our hours together and that, to me, was the proof."

He replied the following day. "Please do not ever say or think that our relationship was responsible for your homosexuality. And please do not ever contact me again."

▲

ON THE DRIVE to his hotel room, I decided that Samuel would

be my last husband.

It was April and I had finally started dating a guy that I liked, a handsome, well-adjusted gay fellow with a sense of humor. But he also lived forty-five minutes away, in the state capitol, so the weeks were sometimes a long stretch of anticipation. Even though I had a rule about not driving to visit a husband, Samuel was different, as gentlemanly as a mayor. And those rules? I think I broke every one.

Samuel lived in a small town three hours to the east of Louisville, where he taught at a Christian College. He'd emailed to ask me out for a drink. Looking back, I'm not sure why I opened myself to his advances. Do we ever completely know the triggers that allow people into our lives? He was in his fifties and his face was lined with the evidence of his youth spent outside on a farm. He had this inexplicably charming Southern twang and bristly moustache. He looked like a bald Captain Kangaroo.

He perched in a hotel chair, one leg thrown over the arm, dressed in drawstring sweatpants and a bright white T-shirt. On the table rested a half-bottle of Coke—no alcohol for him. His eyes had a twinkly devilment, but what kept me parked in the chair was his openness. He was genuine, struggling with his identity, with the possibility of love with a man. Could a man satisfy? Could a man stay? As a teenager, he had fooled around with an older neighbor boy but he'd moved away. His wife, a schoolteacher, had begun to restrict their sex to Saturday and Sunday mornings. With the advent of the Internet, he had met a married "bear" who lived nearby. But after a year, Samuel discovered he was falling in love and told him he was developing "strong feelings." The husband laughed in his face. "He called me a fool," Samuel said. "That hurt me so much, Austin." He kept using my name. I felt like a visiting dignitary.

In retrospect, I want to see this heartbreak as tactic: a story to make me care. But the story was, ultimately, what I was looking for with all these husbands. My father is not a talker, and even though as a college student I once challenged him to explain his infidelities, I don't think I'll ever entirely grasp what his deal was. But Samuel was an English professor. He could tell a story and sweep me up in it. Later, in bed, I'd never seen such delight on a face. His whole body tremored at our contact. As we lay there, I asked him how he squared his religious faith with his homosexuality. Samuel took a deep breath and looked both up and in at the same time. "I believe God has given us the gift of life," he said. "I believe we need to experience that gift as much as possible."

I know what you're thinking. He was unfaithful, a liar, and a mess, like all those husbands. He was a middle-aged man stuck in a transition he did not know how to complete without ruin. But the transition was mine too. Newly single, and no longer young, I'd committed to life on my own terms and my leap year meant a solitude I was unprepared for. I had no idea if this idea of myself would work. Married men validated my freedom without threatening my loyalty, just as I did for them. And when I got up from the bed to leave, I knew I would write all this down, every encounter with every last husband. This was how I'd go forward and break the pattern of giving myself to people who would never give back. I'd put them on the page, just like this, in the past tense.

IN THE BROKENNESS OF SUMMERTIME
R. W. CLINGER

THE SELF-INDUCED CUTS—narrow, razor-sharp lines that proved infidelity, red-purple zigzags against his wrinkled and scarred wrists—would heal Cannon; that is what he often told me. Cutting was significant in his life, a means of his survival, and cutting produced by a tilted marriage was natural medicine, a means of Cannon learning to forgive himself for betraying our Valentine love/lust—something.

The bandages were a logic he used to prevent his insanity. Delicate wrist-armor that he sported almost all the time, never irregularly, keeping the visual atrocity of his sexual desire for another man concealed. And then he covered the bandages with fanciful, almost queer, accessories—a navy-blue scarf, a leather band purchased near the Vista del Rio in Barcelona, a red-white-and-blue bandana—which maybe caused him to believe they had healing powers for both of our hearts, but mostly his.

When his wounds—valley-like gashes at the bottom of both thumbs—were exposed, we were exposed. The lacerations were in view for all to see. Self-incisions because of man-with-man tenderness exposed. Raw tissue of our life together (seventeen years of marriage in Apartment J-1 on Padilla Street, next to the Allegheny River in Pittsburgh) unveiled, the bruised flesh of hardship and indecipherable pain between two men in love. Brokenness was discovered. Those cuts dissected our single unit into two cells: one of faithfulness and the other of radical sin.

Cannon bled.

I was delighted to watch him bleed.

▲

SHRINK TIME.

Estelle listens. It's her job to listen to me once a week, sometimes even twice a week. $150.00 a session. Says that I love Cannon with all my heart. Says we balance each other out. Says it's refreshing for me to call the man a jagged little fuck. Because I hurt. Because Armageddon swooped me up in its hulking arms and gave me a bad ass squeeze. Because Cannon Marshall Dixon could not keep his seven-inch crank inside his running shorts.

And I say to Estelle that it will never be the same between us. Things will always be and feel different. Our gay marriage/companionship/faggot union, or whatever Uncle Sam wants to label it, or not label it, no matter what, the ideal will always be sour. A skim of poison will reside on its surface for years to come, decades.

Estelle says to take a breath. Calm down. I can overcome this challenge.

I reply with something like: Some days I want his cock to fall off. Does that make any sense to you? Is that in your psychology textbooks? Will it ever make any sense to me?

Estelle hits me with a bomb. Psychiatrists can be filthy terrorists in their own little sick ways; any sane patient knows this. She tells me to say his name three times. Do it. Say it three times.

I do. Very fast.

Kyle. Kyle. Kyle.

And I begin to feel better, exposing more of my woe-me pain.

▲

"I SHOULD LEAVE, Cannon. You can have the apartment for yourself."

"Where will you go?"

"My brother's. He has an attic room I can use."

"You need to stay here and we can work this out," Cannon said.

"I'm not sure if I can do that yet. Maybe I need some time alone. I have to heal."

"We can heal together, under the same roof."

"It doesn't work that way. I wished it could, but it won't. We can't even think that will begin to justify my sanity."

⋏

IT HAPPENED LAST summer—what an absurd cliché. The truth, though. The denial of it all. The acceptance on my part that may never happen at all. July. So hot and humid.

Sticky in Pittsburgh, even the bridges were sweating. When pretty boys like Kyle/Kyle/Kyle took off their shirts and exposed their strawberry-colored nipples and blond treasure trails, among other sinful body parts that men in their late forties became quite fond of. Married queer men who desired nothing less than to extend their slippery-naughty tongues and taste those pretty boys. And taste the sweet and refined blend of Kyle Kansas sugar: a steel-plated chest, beam-like shoulders, and comma-shaped navel. Both those men and boys shared grins-a-plenty, but for all the wrong reasons. Relentless sin in the city.

It happened along one of the city's rivers. In the brokenness of summertime, all the rivers looked the same, even to the urbanites. The two men were running together, staying fit.

I didn't know they were horny for each other. Who would have known in my position? I didn't reek of jealousy. But maybe I should have reeked.

They took a sabbatical from their run. And then they crept into the bushes and found themselves against a birch tree, among the honeysuckle and next to a holly bush. A *quickie* was shared, because that's what Cannon labeled the sexual event with Kyle/Kyle/Kyle. They were men who were unseen and unheard in Estarre Park, and communicated by tongue and touch, among other tools.

The details were explicit, which I cared not to know. XXX

stuff that I couldn't deem audible. Two bodies meshed together in the steeping-heat of a July evening. Exercising while exercising.

I shouldn't have been writing, creating, toying with words, sentences, and paragraphs. I should have paid more attention to Cannon, and certainly to the other man. I could have become jealous. I shouldn't have trusted either of them. My clarity was smudged, something I will never forgive myself for. I was a fool being foolish, of course, and maybe part of me deserved that pain.

They broke apart, unhinged from each other's sexual skin. They went to Kyle's place to shower. They showered together, or I told myself that they did. Silence followed that period of space between men who have nothing to say to each other, and men who have too much to say to each other without saying anything at all. A sense of awkwardness was discovered between them. The park-party in their lives had come to an end. Slippage occurred.

Cannon came home; he didn't have to. He could have driven to his sister's in Fox Chapel. He could have spent the night at his uncle's Tudor in Brookline. He could have stayed at the Holiday Inn. But he came home. And he was quiet. Things could break inside the apartment and we were able to hear them break. A wedged soul within a man's torso began to creak. Something was wrong with Cannon. Something had happened. He couldn't hide from me. That wasn't possible.

Then he started to cut himself.

▲

SHRINK TIME.

Estelle asks if I purchase items so Cannon can hurt himself with.

Yes. I won't lie. There's no reason to lie. I've bought a number of tools for his labor of love: Ginzu knives, an ice pick, a few different types of saws, and pocket knives. I am perfectly fine with the man's indulgence and longing that he has to mangle his own skin. It's the little price he has to pay for screwing a guy behind my back.

Estelle mentions that I gift-wrapped a scalpel for my lover.

I don't deny this. Why would I deny this? I tell her it was the perfect little pink present for him. I even added a bow and streamers to it. It was lovely and proved my pain regarding his sexual park-affair. I say to Estelle that I cannot hurt him. This is something he has to accomplish on his own. She gives me a look that says this is fucked up, a tragedy in the making. If I wasn't paying her she would probably think I was to blame for Cannon's affair.

She's silent for a few seconds, perhaps hashes out my situation between her temples and calls my action a projection.

I tell her to explain it to me in layman terms. She defines the condition as Jungian psychology.

She directly stares at me and says that I'm blaming others for my own actions.

I tell her I wasn't the one sucking cock in a park with someone outside my marriage. She doesn't like my tone.

I don't give a fuck what she likes and tell her that she really isn't helping me. I still buy cutting devices for Cannon to use on his wrists. She hasn't convinced me otherwise.

Estelle takes notes, listening to me ramble a list of all the tools I have gifted to my husband since the event in Estarre Park. Estelle stops me. She instructs me to say Kyle/Kyle/Kyle.

I do, without emotion. And now I decide that I am not healed and maybe I don't need her at all. Survival of the fittest comes to mind. Can I pull this off by myself? Maybe I should give it a try.

▲

"I CAN TASTE his cock in your mouth, Cannon. Do you know that?"

"You're being a drama queen. That's absurd."

"I really can. His urine and semen. His saliva and blood. It's all in there."

"You're crazy."

"Crazy in love," I said.

"Call it what you want."

"And to think I'm the demon here, Cannon. To think I was the one who fucked around behind your back. To think I put our relationship in a topsy-turvy spin. Really...Really?"

▲

KYLE WAS CANNON'S student the semester before their shared intimacy. Cannon taught at Pitt: Romanticism, World Literature II, The Critical Approach, A Semester of J. C. Oates, Origins of the English Language. Kyle flirted with my partner. His glinting, hazel-blue eyes must have melted Cannon. The eyes are like that, aren't they? So convincing, spell-concocting, and spoiling. They met for coffee once or twice; a fine line between professor and student was crossed at The Brew Emporium on Beechwood Boulevard. Did the two men—one who looked like a daddy and one who looked like his son—touch fingertips together across a four-person table near the back of the coffee shop? Were winks shared? Did they use the restroom together, pissing side by side and checking out each other's junk?

Nothing ever stops when you want it to; life doesn't function this way. Cannon continued to "see" the student. One short date after the next transpired: evening runs, coffee breaks, and meetings at Turn the Page Books. I was sure they kissed during those brief encounters, mixing lips and mannish body parts. Their conversations were challenging and most interesting; boredom was undiscovered territory.

Their "seeing" progressed into the naked, summertime rendezvous in Esttare Park. Actions I could not fathom, secrets compiled by the two men, filthiness that caused my mind to go numb, semi-paralyzed, and vomit to rise in the narrow passageway of my throat. Their "seeing" was the victorious dilapidation of my heart.

The cutting started after Cannon confessed his infidelity.

I only hoped he would cut out his tongue, saving me from his blunt honesty.

▲

SHRINK TIME.
Estelle reminds me that I hunted Kyle/Kyle/Kyle down like an animal,

hungry to—she looks at her notes on her lap to quote me—eat the home wrecker up and spit him out. She tells me that I followed Kyle for a week and studied his sex-fun with my husband. She says, You wanted to hurt him.

No, I say, I wanted to kill him. A good choking needed to be accomplished, and I was the man to get the job done. He had death coming.

Estelle asks who?

And I scream the guy's name three times at the top of my lungs. After my outburst, she reminds me that I didn't kill Kyle. In fact, you didn't even put a finger on him. I say it was Cannon who prevented me from murdering the once-student. Cannon started cutting himself, which saved me from being incarcerated. What can I say? Cannon had all my attention. No, let me correct that. His cutting had all of my attention, which prompted me to buy things/tools/devices/gadgets/instruments that he could hurt himself with—items I wanted him to own and use on his flesh, mind you. Hell, if I knew he would have used a chainsaw on himself, I would have picked one up at Home Depot or Lowe's. Because deep down inside I wanted that jagged little fuck to cut all of his appendages off, one by one, starting with his dick, of course.

Estelle confirms that I left Kyle alone in hopes that Cannon would mutilate himself.

I reply that this is the truth, and the truth hurts, doesn't it?

Estelle doesn't argue with me, although I expect her to.

⚌

"YOU CAN'T SEE him anymore," I said.

"I didn't say I would."

"You have to promise me to be faithful."

"You don't trust me."

"How can I trust you?" I asked. "You've broken me…us. I see a shrink because of you."

"You don't love me."

"I never said that. You're putting words in my mouth, Cannon."

"We can separate tonight. We'll sleep in different rooms. For once…it will feel right for you. Don't disagree with me, please."

CANNON ENDED THE affair with the other man. I remember the date as if it happened yesterday: December 12, 2011. A date I would never forget, for as long as we were together. He told me to my face that it was over, that he had no interest in Kyle Kansas any longer. He said he loved me, and would always love me, through good and bad. At first, I didn't believe him. Lies upon lies had been built behind my back. Trust between us was untouchable. A fool would have believed him; I had outgrown that position with much skill and ardor. He said his relationship with his former student was severed, completely dissolved. Kyle's telephone number was removed from Cannon's cell phone. No longer was he a friend with Cannon on Facebook. They didn't Tweet each other. Even his e-mail address was deleted from our shared computer and laptop. To think that a delete button could erase the young man from our lives. That happened, though. So easily. So quickly. And I was left bemused because of it.

Cannon was still cutting himself, though. Almost daily. I found the bloody tools in the bathroom. Droplets of rose red blood on a pair of gardening shears. Droplets of crimson-colored blood on a paring knife. Droplets of deep red blood on a pair of vintage nail clippers. He simply left his tools of manipulation behind. Maybe for me to find on purpose. Maybe not. I don't think I'll ever learn the answer to that mystery.

The bandages and accessories still decorated his wrists. He seemed depressed, lost in a world of his own. He was quiet and reserved, which told me that: *Maybe he still loves Kyle. Maybe they are meant to be together. Maybe I'm in the way of things.* I didn't ignore him, although maybe I should have. Things need to be ignored sometimes. Maybe what he was going through was normal. Loss happened. Pain was discovered. I digested that without feeling, and watched him closely.

Six months passed and he was still in a state of depression. He didn't see a therapist, although I had often wanted him to. Cannon kept teaching at Pitt, going to his classes, coming home, and simply dozed away his free time. The man became a vegetable on his own terms: self-blemished, expunged from life, and unremittingly hopeless. Of course I tried to cheer him up. In February, around Valentine's Day, we rented a cabin in the woods for three days; it was freezing and I kept him warm with my bare skin. In April, we drove to Baltimore for a weekend of fun in Little Italy with two other gay couples. In May, we enjoyed Gay Days in downtown Pittsburgh.

The next horrendous episode of our lives happened in June, didn't it, because it was summertime, and he wanted it to happen in June as a symbol of sorts, an underlying perception, encompassing the brokenness of our lives, a sweet summertime evening with purple-red clouds in the sky, a sticky wind, and hungry mosquitoes, the time of day when the city's buildings finally have a shape to them because the sun is perfectly positioned in the sky, hovering.

In June we drove to West Virginia, spent the day gambling, won over two thousand dollars on a quarter machine, and ate at the buffet. That atrocious incident happened almost two hours after we were nestled back home. Smoke-covered from my time in the casino, I showered. What was Cannon doing? I didn't know. He was probably dozing in the spare bedroom, checking his e-mail, or reading a mystery. Maybe I should have known his whereabouts, and then the incident wouldn't have happened. You leave your eyes off the prize for just a second and…it falls away. You lose it. One snap outside the walls of reality and it's fucking gone. Or almost gone. Trust me, I know.

Following my shower, having nothing more than a Martha Stewart towel wrapped around my middle, I looked for him in the apartment: the kitchen, the living room, our bedroom, the spare bedroom. He wasn't anywhere to be found. Did I start to panic? Did something settle underneath my skin that caused me to feel disturbed, lost, confused, and selfless for the first time in my life? Where did Cannon go? What was he up to? Why hadn't he told me he was leaving?

(Kyle/Kyle/Kyle)

The Commander was parked out front, sitting on the street—a mere thirty feet from the apartment building's front door. Maybe Cannon was doing something under its engine. Checking its oil. Writing down its mileage. Looking for its owner's manual. I wasn't sure but wanted to find out. I buzzed through the apartment and looked onto Padilla Street. The car was there, and so was Cannon, slumped over its steering wheel. His neck was arched forward and his forehead was pressed against the black wheel. I called out to him but he didn't answer. I called out a second time, but nothing happened.

The remaining moments of that endeavor were a blur for me for the longest time: slipping into a pair of Rufskin shorts; bolting down the stairs and over the front sidewalk; panting heavily; heart wildly beating within the fold of my chest; pain skiing from one temple to the other temple; yanking the Commander's driver door open; finding Cannon passed out inside the vehicle; the accessories missing from his wrists; both narrow wrists sliced open with the scalpel I gave him as a gift; blood pooling into the Commander's foot well; the scalpel sitting on the passenger seat; the bittersweet stench of thick blood coagulating; the sight of his pallid-white-almost-yellow skin and...

That was his gift to me, I knew. The honesty of his affair, the bridge that would heal our dilapidated relationship. The growth of our togetherness. Simple love found by the attempted act of scalpel-suicide. A magnum deed that would only bring the two of us closer together. He had finally pleased me. I was happy to see him that way. I was thrilled and in love with him again.

All was forgiven, honestly.

▲

SHRINK TIME.

Estelle says Cannon wasn't dead, although he should have been. He didn't kill himself. You called 911 and the paramedics arrived in time.

I say I didn't plan it that way. He deserved to die. We pay for our sins, don't you think? She chooses not to answer me.

Pause. Quiet for the first time since we met. Insanity.

She finally says you saved Cannon's life. You could have left him die, but didn't. You know that. You will always know that. It was the power you had over him. The control. He could have died and you prevented that from happening. It was your means of survival, your devotion to heal because of his affair with Kyle.

I stop listening to her.

She says my name.

I look at her.

Estelle says it's okay to admit that you love him. Your hardship is over. Both of you have survived this. Even the tools are gone. You gave them all away. Anything he could use to cut himself. Everything like that is gone. If you didn't love Cannon you would have kept them. You know this. You can't lie to yourself. This is reality. Kyle is gone. And she tells me to say this three times.

Kyle is gone/Kyle is gone/Kyle is gone.

And I feel better, alive, and a part of Cannon again.

▲

"ARE YOU ASLEEP, Cannon?"

"I was."

"Do you want to sleep?"

"Not anymore. What did you have in mind?"

"Sex, of course," I said.

"The rough and tough stuff?"

"I think I'd like that."

"You're demented," he said.

"And you love that about me."

Any Resemblance to Actual Persons, Living or Dead, Is Entirely Coincidental
Tom Mendicino

IT WAS A Monday in early May, my last night in North Carolina before moving back to Philadelphia to study for the bar exam. I'd loved my three years as a Tar Heel, but I'd made a bargain with my partner of almost ten years after the law school at Chapel Hill accepted me. He would remain in Pennsylvania practicing medicine while I went out-of-state to study, and I would return to the City of Brotherly Love when I graduated. The year I left Philadelphia, 1985, was the height of the epidemic, a horror we had witnessed up close and personal, as Nick, my partner, was (and is) a physician and had been an AIDS activist before the disease had even been given a name. It was one of the rare times in history when it seemed easy and desirable for gay men to be relatively monogamous. Watching friends you loved die ugly and painful deaths didn't exactly inflame the libido. Under the circumstances, the challenges of maintaining a long-distance relationship didn't seem to be a serious threat to our relationship.

Still, I was a young man with a surplus of hormones and stress and loneliness can be a powerful antidote to a repressed sex drive. On a rainy December night, before my labor law exam during my second year, opportunity first presented itself on a commercially undeveloped strip of highway close to RDU

International Airport, the perfect location for a barebones cinderblock facility whose discreet signage, ADULT MOVIES, was barely visible from the access road. The clientele of the Aphrodite Bookstore ranged from the stunning to the grotesque, from grizzled mechanics and warehousemen to traveling salesmen to nervous frat boys and suburban dads, all looking for a quick release—jack, wipe, and run. At any time of the day or night you'd find pickup trucks and family sedans and delivery vans in the parking lot. No names, no numbers, no personal information, and, for me at least, no bodily fluids were exchanged. I'd discovered a reasonable compromise to enforced celibacy, anonymous and safe, neither an emotional or physical threat to my relationship.

The rental truck was packed by nine; my buddy, Pat, who was driving north with me, suggested we go out for a few beers. I shrugged and declined, pleading an early morning and a long day's drive ahead of us. We said goodnight and ten minutes later I was headed to the Aphrodite for a farewell tour among the maze of peep booths. My first glimpse of the man who would inspire a story that would change my life was a white shirttail, bright as a floodlight in the dimly lit arcade. His Madras shorts seemed out of place and the rubber soles of his boat shoes squeaked as he pivoted and disappeared. I turned the corner just in time to see him slip into a booth. I heard the jangle of tokens dropping, followed by the exaggerated moans of a woman begging her partner to fuck her tight pussy. The adjacent stall was empty so I sat down, shut the door, and leaned forward to peer through the glory hole. He was sprawled spread-eagled on the seat. A stubby but plump cock, fully erect, poked through his open fly. When I slipped two fingers through the glory hole, he jumped to his feet, pulled up his zipper and slammed the door behind him.

I bolted from my booth, intending to chase him, and stood face-to-face with a scrawny, ginger-haired kid in a UNC tee shirt. I pushed his hand away when he grabbed my crotch, interested only in pursuing the man who'd just rejected me. I made a quick dash through the deserted maze. Only one red "occupied" door light was lit in the entire arcade. I leaned against the wall, doing my best James Dean imitation, certain the man in the Madras shorts and boat shoes would soon emerge. After a seeming eternity, the door swung open and an enormous black man with a shaved head and a Mr. Clean earring stepped out of the booth. He barely acknowledged me as he tossed a wet, sticky tissue on the floor. Disheartened, I did one final walkthrough. The only patrons left in the Aphrodite were me and the skinny college kid who was standing in the corner, his pants and underwear around his ankles, furiously pounding his flaccid cock. It was time to call it a night, the last roundup at the Aphrodite having been a crushing disappointment.

Stepping out into the humid night air, I shivered despite the heat, tingling with that strange sensation that ripples up your spine when you actually feel someone staring at you. I turned and got my first good look at the man in the Madras shorts. Tall, broad-shouldered, strapping, he looked like he'd once been an athlete, a high school tight end or wrestler, floppy-haired, a real boy, a true Son of the South. He was standing beside a very expensive import, a white BMW sports coupe. He smiled, slowly opened the door of his car, slipped behind the wheel and opened the window. I saw the flame of his match as he lit a cigarette. And there he sat, blowing smoke rings out of the car.

I was usually pretty reticent in situations like that, assuming rejection, but that night I was full of bravado, knowing this was a rare opportunity and that I would regret slinking away without seizing the moment. I walked over to the car and extended my hand. We introduced ourselves. His name was Hal—an acronym of his initials—and he invited me back to his place for a drink. Five minutes later, I was following him in my car, driving blind on some county road in Wake County, no idea where we were going.

Finally, we entered a sprawling, well-lit gated community— I'd never seen a gated community before—and pulled up in front of a big, beautiful new townhouse. He wanted me to park by the curb, not in the driveway. He hustled me along, waving his hand as I got out of the car, looking this way and that, making sure no one was watching. He opened the front door and told me to go inside. I took about three steps down the dark hallway and fell flat on my face.

I'd tripped over one of those baby car seats. Hal told me his wife was six months pregnant. She and her mother had gone to New York on a shopping trip and left him alone all week. He said he didn't get a lot of opportunities like this, to spend a little of what he called "guy time." Hal said he really loved his wife, was looking forward to starting a family, that there was nothing in his life he wanted to change. It was just that sometimes he felt something was missing, that sex with his wife was never as exciting as it was with a man.

I wasn't the type of man who was turned off by such revelations. In fact, the idea of fucking a woman's husband under her roof was wildly titillating. I assumed the rest of the house was off limits. I expected he was going to offer a quick blowjob in the living room, maybe jack off into his fist with my dick in his mouth. I resigned myself to having taken a long detour into the dark hinterlands of suburban Raleigh-Durham for what promised to be a five-minute encounter. We could have pulled off this little quickie in a booth at the Aphrodite, saving me a quarter tank of gas. So I was startled when he grabbed my face with his hands and kissed me. He whimpered as I sucked his tongue; I could feel his erection as he grabbed me by the waist and ground his hips against my crotch.

"Come upstairs," he said as he took me by the hand and led me up the staircase. A bedside lamp was lit in what was clearly the master bedroom. His wife had learned her decorating skills from the pages of *Southern Living*. A woman's touch was evident in the swag curtains, the ruffled bed skirt, and the collection of vanilla-scented candles. He carefully folded the quilted comforter, piled the decorative throw pillows on a plush armchair beside the window, and then politely excused himself and closed the bathroom door behind him.

I sat on the edge of the bed, a bit unnerved by his disappearance. I considered leaving before he returned, but I had a raging erection and a burning curiosity to see how this strange and unexpected evening would play out. I stripped to my boxers and stretched out on the mattress, waiting. I heard water splashing in the sink; he gargled and spit. He finally emerged, wearing nothing but a pair of white briefs. His body was well defined without being chiseled. His chest was smooth, with flat brown nipples the size of silver dollar pancakes. A faint trail of hair snaked above the elastic waistband of his Jockey shorts, fading just below his navel.

The bedsprings creaked as he lowered himself onto the mattress. We lay side by side, staring at each other for a long, quiet moment, and then he leaned forward and kissed me. He came quickly after I touched him, still wearing his underpants. I expected him to turn away, dismiss me in a sudden rush of guilt, but instead he rolled me on my back and stripped off my boxers. His tongue gradually worked its way from my sweaty armpits to my belly to my raging erection. He yanked off his briefs and threw a leg over my waist, straddling me as he grabbed my cock to guide it into his ass. As he lowered his hips onto my penis, I gently pushed him away.

"Put a rubber on it," I whispered.

"Okay," he said, deftly balancing himself on his heels, assuming I was going to hand him a condom.

"Don't worry about it," he said after we ascertained neither of us had come prepared. "Just pull out before you come."

I hadn't had any unsafe encounters since my HIV test a few months ago. I was sure a suburban husband about to become a father had to be clean. There was a one in ten million chance of transmitting the virus between us, I guessed. But I thought about the fresh-faced young bride in the wedding pictures on the mantel downstairs and the child she was carrying. I figured

Hal was naïve, living in a safe, sequestered bubble, unaware of the potential consequences of what he suggested. It didn't seem worth even the slimmest of risks to me.

"Sorry," I said. "Maybe next time."

He didn't seem terribly disappointed, telling me he knew plenty of other ways to get me off. I had two orgasms and he came a second time before the pale gray light of dawn began to brighten the room. He laughed and offered to call out from work; he had plenty of unused sick time. I was tempted to encourage him, but knew that Pat was already stirring, anxious to get on the road, wondering where I'd disappeared to, waiting for me to return from my nocturnal prowl. Hal insisted I stay for a cup of coffee. We stood in the kitchen, me fully dressed, he in his tidy whities, and made small talk. He gave me his business card, saying it was okay to call him at work. I said goodbye reluctantly and promised to stay in touch. He had one last question to ask before I left. Did I know Clayton Ross? Clayton Ross—a pseudonym, of course—was a red-faced blowhard in my graduating class. He prided himself on his provincial bigotry, once asking me for advice on how to behave after he'd agreed to go on a date with a *Catholic girl.*

"He likes to get fist-fucked," Hal confided, the bitter undertone hinting at some unresolved anger. "I fucked him in his mother's basement all through high school."

I never saw him again after that night. I called him once, at his office. He sounded nervous and said he'd be there after five. Could I call back then, after everyone else was gone? "We can talk dirty," he said, "and jack off to the sound of each other's voice." No one answered when I called at the appointed hour. I never tried again. But I would think of him often, whenever I'd encounter some married man in town on business, attending a convention, holed up in a hotel room, looking to scratch an itch. Or whenever I'd pick up the paper and read about another politician, usually some evangelical Republican, caught in a stall in a public bathroom.

I published my first novel, *Probation*, in 2010. It had been a long journey from my undergraduate years at the University of Pennsylvania in the 1970's when mentors like the novelists Mark Harris and Jerre Mangione had first encouraged my writing ambitions. Mark Harris had gone so far as to introduce me to his agent, who wisely declined to represent a hotheaded young smart ass who blithely rejected her suggestions to improve my obviously perfect and brilliant manuscript. I didn't sit down to write again for nearly twenty-five years when, on a whim, I decided to try to record some of the stories that were banging around in my fevered imagination.

As a fledgling writer who had already entered middle age, I wasn't endlessly fascinated with the myth of my own history, self-absorption being the folly of a younger man. It was other people's stories that engaged me, usually tales concocted whole cloth out of snippets of overheard conversations, assumptions and predictions determined by me to be the absolute truth. One story that continued to intrigue me was Hal's. How had he ended up in his marriage? Where had his life taken him? Was he still hiding in the closet? Or had he eventually come out and, if so, how and why? How had his life's decisions affected his wife and child (or children)?

The story of my protagonist Andy Nocera, a married man kicked to the curb by his wife after being arrested giving a blowjob at an interstate rest area, wasn't *based* on Hal's life experience. Having spent only a few hours with him on that single night, Hal's biography was unknown to me. I knew nothing about his life before his marriage except for that one strange and unexpected disclosure about a despised classmate. I knew nothing about his relationship with his wife—how they met, the things they shared, what they talked about, any of their plans and dreams other than that they were expecting a child. I didn't even know her name. I could only guess at what he did for a living from the information on the business card he handed me.

Any resemblance to actual persons, living or dead, is entirely coinciden-

tal wasn't simply legal jargon to protect me and my publisher from legal action. It was the honest to God truth. But my last night in North Carolina clearly *inspired* the novel. If I'd never met Hal, my first novel would have been a very different book from *Probation*.

After the book was published, I was asked to speak at the opening of the new GLBT library in Raleigh. I was deeply touched to be invited back to North Carolina as an honorary native son. Old friends from law school would be attending and we decided to make it a "homecoming" weekend. On a whim, I Googled Hal's name, fully expecting the closest hit to be a solicitation for one of those bogus sites that promise to find anybody, anywhere for a nominal fee charged to a major credit card. Much to my surprise, I discovered two intriguing clues. The first hit was a ten-year old appellate court decision in a criminal case. Hal had been the star witness, the victim of a non-violent crime. Hal's male "roommate" also provided evidence that had helped to convict the defendant.

The second hit was of a more recent vintage. In fact, it was current. His LinkedIn profile indicated that Hal was working for himself now, apparently the sole proprietor of a Raleigh retail business located only a few blocks away from where I would be speaking. For several days, I entertained a wild fantasy. I would inscribe a copy of *Probation* and personally deliver it to his business address, unannounced. I would invite him and his "roommate" to the reading, introduce them to the audience if they didn't mind a bit of local notoriety. Afterwards, we could go out for drinks and share notes comparing how Hal and Andy Nocera became the men they were always destined to be. But reality grounded me soon enough and I expected that Hal wouldn't even recall our one night together. I could expect a blank look at best. The worst-case scenario might be he'd think I was some lunatic who'd wandered in off the street and ask the security guard to escort me to the door.

I did call the business number listed and even used my actual name when I asked to speak to Hal. I wondered if I would recognize his voice after all the intervening years. He said hello, sounding no different than any other native of the North Carolina Piedmont, speaking with the soft, understated accent of mythical Mayberry. My name meant obviously nothing to him; he pleasantly asked how he could help me and seemed surprised that I'd needed to speak directly to him just to ask the hours of operation. "Ten to seven, Monday through Saturday," he said, "twelve to five on Sunday."

I politely thanked him and hung up. I thought about stopping in the store when I was in town and making a small purchase. Yet, in the end, I decided the wiser choice was to remember Hal as he had once been, the floppy-haired young man, not yet middle-aged, blowing smoke rings out of his car window, the inspiration for my own Andy Nocera.

COMPLICITY
MARK CANAVERA

EVEN TODAY, NEITHER of us knows who cheated first. The moments of discovery—those piercing, icicle moments when the world goes white noise and the senses throb—*those* we know. The subsequent accusations and investigations, the self-flagellation that occurs when piecing together the shards of events—*those* we can recall. But we never attempted to tie together the strands of our twin infidelities to create a single narrative with mutually agreed meanings. There probably is no sense to be made from the overlapping layers of lies.

I learned about Ousmane's indiscretions on the morning after my thirty-second birthday. We were sitting on the balcony of my apartment, drinking coffee and talking through his activities for the coming day. I left him on the balcony, sat down at the kitchen table, and opened my computer, where I found his email account left open from the previous evening. He had been drafting the following: "You are the only one who loves me. Without you, I am nothing."

I smiled, thinking the message was an unfinished birthday wish addressed to me. Then I noticed the intended recipient: Anthony Antreux. I copied Anthony's email address and searched for it among Ousmane's messages. There were scores of messages, dating back months; I forwarded each one to myself, methodically, deleted these forwarded messages from his "sent mail" folder, closed his account, closed my computer, and joined my love back on the balcony. I sipped my coffee and tried to will away the pounding in my ears. We chatted. He left. I began reading, email after gory email. Ousmane started most of the messages with, "You are the only one who loves me," or "You are the only person left for me." So who was I? Who were any of us in this tawdry micro-drama?

The scene was 2009, Abidjan, the magnetic metropolis of French-speaking West Africa and the economic capital of Côte d'Ivoire, a country besieged by a decade-long armed conflict that left its once-strong economy in tatters. Ousmane is Ivoirian; at the time, he was a door-to-door clothing and fragrance salesman, peddling merchandise imported from France in government offices and upscale neighborhoods. I am an American who has spent most of his adult life in West Africa. In 2009, I was about a decade into my career, working with a large international organization and shuttling between Côte d'Ivoire's South, still ruled by the government, and the North, whose administration was made up of rebel forces.

Daily life in Abidjan, which is located on the southern coast, was essentially militarized with rampant road blocks and extortionary police checks—Kalashnikovs strung across men's backs on many corners. In another way, though, life just went on. Abidjan's denizens themselves soldiered on, buying their morning baguettes and croissants, commuting to work, making daily market trips, filling nightclubs to overflowing on weekends, normalizing and humanizing what might have become an unlivable environment. Abidjan is skyscrapers and highways, but the guidebooks were beginning to call it "tattered" and "dog-eared." One book depicted the city as "a shadow of its former self."

The shadows of war were heavy, and I myself was gearing up for battle. I felt armed: Ousmane's emails were bullets of truth that I was loading into my revolver's chamber for an eventual reckoning. I read and re-read them, but one sentence really stood out: "You are the only one who loves me." It was a personal affront. Anthony, I would learn through Facebook and Google searches, was a successful French businessman in his fifties who shared his time between Paris and Miami, often with his wife. "You are the only one who loves me." The sentence seared. It showed up my inadequacies as a lover; it made me feel useless and small, much the same way I suppose Ousmane had felt when he learned about my own act of infidelity some two months prior. Ousmane's revelation had come one night that he was out to dinner with friends. I had hooked up with Thierry, a gay filmmaker and lead character in Abidjan's small circles. (Homosexuality is not illegal in Côte d'Ivoire, as it is in many African countries, but people who reveal their alternative sexualities to family and friends nonetheless often face family rejection and social marginalization.) The filmmaker had begun gossiping about our tryst, news of which rippled in a matter of days to Ousmane. When he heard, he called me from the restaurant where he and his friends were eating. "Where were you on Thursday night? They're telling me that Thierry was in your room, but I've told them you would never do that to me. I've told them you are not like other white men." I failed to fib my way through the conversation.

Ousmane did not file away his newfound information in a methodical, calculated way, as I would do in later months with his emails. Rather, by the end of the evening, Ousmane was in my apartment with bleeding knuckles and alcohol on his breath. He had tracked down Thierry in a bar; fisticuffs had ensued. Thierry, who had not fared well in the battle, was threatening to press charges. Witnesses to the event told me later that any doubts about Ousmane's love for me could be laid to rest. "He loves you; he really loves you." I wavered between my aspirational pacifism and some unearned primordial pride. My man had defended me, even if I did not merit the defense.

Ousmane sat on my bedside, head in hands, sobbing. "How could you do this to me, Mark? I thought you were different." So had I. In that moment, my love for Ousmane surged. He slept in my bed that night, knotted into a tiny ball. The following day, I took him to a doctor's clinic, where they patched up his hand and told him he was stressed. We went to a nearby restaurant; I smoked and drank coffee while Ousmane recounted the previous night's events, blow by literal blow, in between bites of rotisserie chicken. There was no pride—rather sadness, confusion, bewilderment, and humiliation. He finished his lunch; I dropped him off at his apartment and went to my office. I never spoke to Thierry again.

Somehow we muddled through. I don't know why Ousmane chose to forgive me or when he stopped holding my feet to the fire. When, in the earliest days of our relationship, I would ask Ousmane what he looked for in a partner, he always answered with the same word: complicity. He wanted an accomplice in life. I had dreamed of being that accomplice—what a marvelous worldview: Life as an obstacle course with paired teams scheming to navigate and overcome—but then I opted out of the game. Both of us were mourning the loss of the sense that we would tackle the world together. I was grateful for forgiveness.

Then I found the emails. The simplest of analyses put Ousmane's lovesick missives to Anthony starting around the time that he and I met. "You are the one person left for me." I kept reading, searching between the lines for hints about their relationship. There were few. The emails were mostly fluffy declarations of love with no there there. The emails did reveal that Anthony's wife, also French, was aware of some of his past dalliances with African men and was trying to clamp down, seemingly halfheartedly. In some emails, Ousmane put in requests for T-shirts and cologne deliveries. Was Anthony also a partner in Ousmane's business endeavors? What kinds of conversations were they having now, during this period in which I built up my arsenal and made sure that the dossier was as complete as possible before presenting Exhibit A? What of the fact that I had undertaken reconnaissance on Ousmane's email account, even if I hadn't gone to extreme lengths to snoop?

Would this evidence be permissible in a jury of our peers? Probably not, but that didn't make the information untrue. I pontificated and smoked and stayed late at the office.

I ended my relationship with Ousmane by telephone. I called him from the airport as I left to Senegal for a short work trip. I didn't tell him why, perhaps because I didn't know myself. I did not present him with the dossier for the time being; rather, I spoke platitudes, calmly. "We have different values," and "We are at different stages in our lives."

He replied calmly, "I can tell you've thought a lot about this."

The explosions came upon my return to Abidjan from Senegal one week later, when I laid out what I had learned on the first day of my thirty-second birthday. I pulled out my revolver and fired each bullet of "truth"—each one carefully stored, preserved, and caressed—straight at Ousmane. He took the hits and came back swinging. He was initially angry that I had read his private emails. I ceded the point but reiterated that the facts remained intact. Eventually, Ousmane agreed that he had wronged me but never that he had cheated on me. Anthony, he explained, was a naïve, long-distance sugar daddy who—without ever having met Ousmane—was willing to send him money and gifts. The explanation made Ousmane a scam artist and fools out of me and Anthony, but from Ousmane's perspective, I had committed the greater transgression: I had brought another man into my bed while his relationship with Anthony remained virtual. "He's seen your sex, Mark. You don't think that's worse?"

I resumed a life of living room socials and became a regular at Abidjan's single gay bar, where young gay men could replicate Beyoncé's "Single Ladies" video to perfection. I lamented my fate to any of our mutual friends who would give me an ear. My hypocrisy was appalling.

You spend a brutal period sifting and sorting the puzzle pieces, trying to figure out what went wrong. But when two partners in a couple have both cheated, the soul-searching becomes redundant and eventually feels beside the point. Time-lines cease to matter. Explanations can only come up short.

The explanations are the funny part; I have cut both Ousmane's and mine every which way, and none of them bear much scrutiny. They are justifications. The Latin root of the word "justify"—*justificare*—means not only "to bring to trial" but also "to make just" or "to do right." But our justifications, shameless and self-serving, were not moving us toward any kind of righteousness or justice. They were nothing but excuses.

▲

WAR CHANGES EVERYTHING. I moved back to the United States in early 2010, exhausted by the treadmill work cycle of humanitarian aid, squeezed dry from the expatriate life, and convinced that I might "find myself" if I reintegrated my own culture after my lost twenties. I continued consulting on humanitarian projects and traveling to some degree. I volunteered at the local HIV/AIDS support center in my hometown, where I soaked up stories of the Gay Old South from a middle-aged queen who shared stories of farm-field romps in Virginia and chocolate shops and teardrops in Charleston, South Carolina.

Younger gay men organized a social group at the center, and I watched their highfalutin' drama with bemused weariness and latent jealousy. Having spent the lion's share of my twenties in Africa, and now into my thirties, I had to wonder what developmental steps I might have missed in becoming a full-blooded queer. Of course, I had my own war stories to tell. My first partner had been an illiterate construction worker from Burkina Faso whose laughter could unhinge doors. I had also lived in a rebel town, where dance-floor gyrations might reveal pistols packed into belt loops and back pockets; where night-club sparkles might be reflecting the disco ball or golden teeth or the lamé tops of the fierce prostitutes; where the months prior to my arrival in 2007 had been witness to anti-gay programs. Yes, I had stories, but mine were exotic. I felt out of place in the States.

War changes everything. By early 2011, one year on from my departure, Côte d'Ivoire had descended from tension and sporadic violence—a situation that the United Nations dubbed "no peace, no war"—into all-out war. I had spoken to Ousmane only once in the intervening year to present my condolences at the death of his father in late 2010. But then warfare reached our beloved Abidjan. The city once known as "Little Paris" was under siege, and Ousmane was living right through it. Somehow the cell phone lines remained operational.

There is little to talk about with a person living through war other than the war itself. I called every day and heard stories about dwindling water supplies and shooting in the streets. With time, Ousmane came to talk about his father—how much he missed him and wished that he were there to comfort and to advise. But then food rations would usurp the reverie. "I'm hungry." Speaking to someone you once loved—or that you love—and hearing about suffering that you can in no way relieve is eviscerating. "I'm hungry. I'm hungry. I'm hungry."

Eventually, if they are not to metastasize, infidelities must be laid to rest. The parties must declare a truce; they must lay down their weapons. There is not any other way to cure them. The real bullets ripping the air in Abidjan and the tanks rending the streets gave Ousmane and me the opportunity to make peace. The trivialities shatter into dust, and one question stares you down: Are we complicit? Ousmane and I had been complicit in dishonesty. What remained to be seen was whether we could be complicit in seeking higher truths, waging peace, loving each other.

I remember a discussion from my early years in West Africa, when I was a Peace Corps volunteer in Burkina Faso. Ousmane grew up in Burkina Faso, which borders Côte d'Ivoire to the North; the two countries share deep historical, socio-political, cultural, and economic roots. One of the Peace

Corps staff members, Cathy—a caring, bespectacled teacher who had learned the difficult skill of explaining one's own culture to misguided but well-intentioned outsiders—was talking me through her views on unfaithfulness.

After living three years in Burkina Faso, I continued to struggle when confronted with situations of infidelity. My understanding, and one that Cathy encouraged, was that the expected and respectful *modus operandi* for reacting to situations where I learned that one partner in a couple had been unfaithful was to keep my big mouth shut. "But what if I'm close to the wife while the husband is cheating flagrantly? What if he's sleeping with her friend?" I implored. I encountered these situations then, and I still do—in West Africa and in the United States, where I live now. My urge to squeal, to proclaim "truths," to gossip has subsided over the years.

"The truth isn't important," my Peace Corps mentor assured me. "Reconciliation is important." That seeped in.

Let's return to those excuses, the ones that Ousmane and I proffered feebly, each in turn. I have come to think that the substance of the excuses themselves has little bearing. What matters is the intent. In our worst moments, we offer excuses in an effort to shift blame—the "you" excuses. "You weren't satisfying me sexually," or "You were emotionally distant," or "You didn't meet my needs." These excuses are weak-willed, cowardly, and I have probably spoken each of them.

But perhaps there is another kind of excuse, still self-serving but more humane. The Latin root of the word "excuse" is *excusare*, meaning, literally, "to free from a charge." The French word *excuser* grew out of this definition, meaning, "to forgive." I am not yet convinced that this form of excuse exists vis-à-vis infidelity, but it just might: These forms of excuses might be the genuine "I" excuses: "I was trying to make my life work." "I was lost." "I don't know." And I don't, but I do know that excuses are more comforting when they are rooted in remorse.

TURBULANCE
CHUCK WILLMAN

WE MET IN a men's room deep under the belly of Chicago's O'Hare International Airport, a sacred sanctuary where horny men came to pray to Pan, or other gods, drawn like bees to honey in this beguiling bastion for desperate deviants. Wedding rings and identities slipped off with the simple closing of a stall's stainless steel door. There was more toe tapping than a road company of *42nd Street* on the shiny linoleum floor soiled with enough spilled DNA to keep a crime lab busy for days. Those of us lucky to find an open stall scurried in and locked ourselves in, then waited like concubines until our legs went numb. It was the early 1990's and some of us were still playing Russian roulette. Our arrows were always cocked and aimed, but some were poisoned. I think a lot of us pretended and believed we were "innocent" and that *safer sex* was basically all we could get away with in rooms like this.

The bustling room finally cleared, leaving two of us sitting in adjacent stalls. Slowly, the massive metal toilet paper dispenser swung on its long, industrial hinge into my stall. The occupant was framed like a Mapplethorpe photograph and stood still like an offering with a perfect portrait of a penis. Mocha-colored, thick, veined and the fat head sheathed in supple foreskin hanging from the open fly of navy blue trousers. His heavy dark testicles bobbed freely as he aroused both himself and me by tugging and stretching his lengthy hood. I dropped to my knees as if praying to a shrine, and then reached around to grab his marble-solid butt, pulling the rising erection firmly into my mouth and latching on like a hungry baby to its mother's nipple. Soon he braced against the cold steel wall, blasting warm semen into my throat.

He squatted to face me, smiling and gazing into my eyes before holding my slimy chin in his hand, leaning forward to kiss and lick my mouth clean, like a lioness after her cub had fed. "Open your door," he whispered, shuffling into my stall, his trousers still puddled around his ankles. We stood face to face, sans shyness or remorse. He was another flight attendant killing time like I was before his next flight, and trying desperately to keep his uniform clean.

"You're beautiful," he said. He reached forward and held me in his thick, Mexican, body-builder arms, and everything moved in slow motion, like Tony and Maria at the dance. And while our space was limited, our imagination and lust were not. We managed to make love quietly and tenderly this time within the stall's walls.

After we left the stall—eyeing each other in the mirrors above the sinks and snickering like kids as we washed up—he scribbled "Mario" and his phone number on a scrap of paper towel. He insisted I call him when he got home from his trip. He held and kissed me again, right in the open as a businessman entered the restroom. It was clear Mario wasn't intimidated by anyone, and I felt a strange comfort and safety with him, mixed with the excitement of it all. We went our separate ways, glancing back to smile, both of us already saddened by the distance. *A fluke: a connection in a toilet stall.* I felt like a kid who had made a new best friend on the first day of school.

Nervous and anxious, I called. He invited me to meet him in a hotel for a weekend where we would have privacy and more comfortable, sanitary conditions. Thinking only of his beautiful, magnificent body and all the possibilities it held, I agreed. We ravaged each other like cannibals, as if we could eat our way to each other's hearts. We made wild, passionate love, instinctually knowing what the other desired as if we had been lovers for years. For weeks we met. I traveled to where he lived just to stay up all night so we could feast on one another. In my mind I had found the perfect mate.

After six weeks, my therapist at the time put an abrupt end to my fantasy life, pointing out the myriad list of lies and blurred lines I had crossed in my quest for carnal bliss. She convinced me I had no choice but to come clean.

Days later, before Mario boarded his plane for a long international flight, my hand quivered as I presented him with my carefully crafted six-page confessional letter in a sealed envelope. Scheduled for a two-day layover before working his flight back, I gave him strict instructions not to read it until he was in the privacy of his hotel room, after he'd relaxed with a cocktail or two. With a bewildered look on his face, he slowly took the envelope from me and placed it in his crew bag. I did my best to pretend it was nothing, maybe my version of a send-off love letter. But I could see in his big brown eyes that he knew *something* was going on. I just hoped and prayed he would appreciate my candor and forgive me.

As the rest of his 747 crew started walking past the gate in a single file line, Mario kissed me goodbye and looked deep into my eyes as if searching for some secret clue in them. But it was time to go, so he quickly turned, giving me a final wave, then headed down the jetway.

▲

BEFORE ALL OF this happened, I had left a career as a television makeup artist in Los Angeles to become a flight attendant. It was a rather sudden decision, but I was ready to leave the rat race of Hollywood behind, and I had always dreamed of flying and having the ability to travel and not be tied down. In 1988 I met and began dating Jerry, a great guy in the small city where I was based after I began my new career flying. Soon, I became rather serious with Jerry. I wanted to keep my options open and also missed L.A. and the friends I had there, and I went back and forth in my mind whether to return. I enjoyed my new profession, but I wasn't crazy about living in the Midwest.

One of Jerry's ex-lovers had been living with AIDS for a few years, though he remained relatively healthy. One night I asked Jerry if he thought it was important for everyone (meaning *me*) to be tested for HIV. (Jerry was already being routinely tested, as he was involved in a study at the Howard Brown Clinic in Chicago, and he always tested negative despite a sexual history not unlike mine.) At the time I didn't think I had anything to worry about. I was convinced I was somehow shielded from infection, maybe even omnipotent, so I went to the local HIV/AIDS clinic in the small city in Indiana where I was living for my 'anonymous' test.

I managed to keep my cool for three days waiting for my test results, though I did try to put together a mental list of what I had done and with whom during my years in Los Angeles. But I was convinced I had nothing to worry about. The day arrived when I would get my results back, and I sat quietly in a counselor's office, staring at my watch as I was scheduled to fly a trip that morning and needed to be on my way to the airport. I assumed I'd get the safe-sex speech, an armful of pamphlets and other "goodies" to use in the future, along with my *negative* test results. But the room spun as the counselor's voice grew soft and he opened a manila folder and apologetically announced that my test had come back *positive. I was HIV-POSITIVE.* I sat in shock and disbelief, staring out the window at a crisp October sky, mesmerized by the gold and orange leaves fluttering in the breeze on a tree framed by the window. My mind went blank, as if it had completely shut down. I was numb, dumbfounded. *DOOMED!* I don't recall hearing anything else the counselor said to me in his soothing, almost monotone voice. All I remember was thinking my life was over. My luck had run out.

Testing positive for HIV in 1988 obviously changed my life. The epidemic had killed thousands of people by then, and since I was now infected, it was essential to take better care of myself in order to survive. Often I felt like a rat running non-stop on a wheel, getting nowhere. But like most "poz" folks back then, AZT became a daily part of my life, as it was the only drug approved and available. Unfortunately it also meant making some major adjustments for some unpleasant and inconvenient side effects. In a short time, the AZT took a serious toll on my body as I was away from home so often, flying long days one after the other on a regular basis. Dealing with the emotional turmoil of the disease and an uncertain future were certainly the most frightening aspects of being HIV-positive. However, I was fortunate to have found a wonderful therapist who specialized in cancer patients and others struggling with terminal illness. HIV/AIDS was still considered "terminal" in 1988. What I *wasn't* dealing with very well was how HIV required me to change my sexual behavior. My appetite for sex and affection actually increased, though I was playing with poisoned darts. I wasn't doing anything to put others *knowingly* "at risk," but I wasn't abstaining, either. To my therapist, this triggered a "red flag." I was not only playing with fire, but my arrows were both flaming and poisoned with the potential to be deadly.

After seeing my therapist a couple times a week for several weeks, she referred me to a psychiatrist for further evaluation. She had a sneaking suspicion that I wasn't simply depressed or "distraught" over my HIV diagnosis, but based on my family history and other factors, she'd observed symptoms of *bipolar disorder*. The psychiatrist quickly came to the same conclusion. I had all the classic symptoms of the disorder: deception to others and myself; delusions of grandeur; my mouth not being able to keep up with my brain; and seeking a sexual "high" that couldn't be satisfied. I was attempting to live at least two lives at the same time. I was diagnosed with bipolar II, along with what is known as "rapid cycling" where moods could turn on a dime, which helped to explain some of my behaviors. I was prescribed Lithium immediately and continued therapy. And for the first time in several years I actually felt like a real human being.

I was still seeing Jerry and had fallen deeply in love with him. We had been dating for several months, and I moved in with him when he bought his first house. I assumed this solidified our commitment to one another, and we'd live *happily ever after*. But shortly after we built our little love-nest, our sex suddenly changed. Jerry was supportive and caring, but I often felt a growing distance between us physically. I lacked the skills to really *communicate* with him about my needs or listen to his. Jerry would masturbate often, rather than have any sexual contact with me. He would jerk off right before I got home from my trips, making me feel as though *that* part of our relatively new relationship was somehow off limits and that my presence for his sexual satisfaction was definitely not required. So, out of physical need, and perhaps a little revenge, I had *"safer"* sex with strangers while out of town on layovers.

▲

WHAT I CONFESSED in the letter I had painstakingly written and handed to Mario before his flight that day were essential facts I had conveniently omitted about myself. At that time I was swept up in a romance that I thought would "fix me." But the reality was I didn't want to face the truth that I was already in a relationship of two years, and I was HIV-positive, vital facts I had not disclosed to Mario. This made me a liar, adulterer, and *poisoned goods*. I even attempted to explain my bipolar illness to him. I wanted Mario not to blame me for withholding the truth. I wrote that I wished I had been honest from the start, but I didn't know how to extinguish the raging fire of passion that truly burned out of control. I had never felt that kind of intensity before—a deep connection with someone else, even though

I had been dishonest from the beginning. I wrote how much I cared for him and how important he was to me. And in the last sentence I had the gall to ask that we continue our affair as if nothing had changed! I had already decided to leave Jerry and move to Chicago, regardless of Mario's decision. At the time I wrote that letter, my relationship with Jerry felt like a dead end, and I believed I would be happier in a big city again.

When I phoned Mario a few days later, he was obviously hurt and extremely angry. I pleaded with him to meet one last time so I could explain and apologize in person. Surprisingly, he agreed, and I flew to Chicago to meet him. I was shocked at how sweet and kind he was upon seeing me again, even accepting part of the blame—my luck and consolation prize—as he listened to my "reasons" like a pitch over a meal he couldn't eat in a small restaurant where we sat at a dark corner table.

He cried and finally asked, "How could you have been so cruel playing with my emotions when I cared for and trusted you so much?" He even told me that he had fallen in love with me, which felt like a dagger in my heart. Then, after dinner, we went back to his apartment and I slept with him one more night; we made love one last time with a sad tenderness, both of us knowing it was the last time we would see one another. I knew it was my parting gift, and it would have to be enough. I had to face my fears and move on.

With my tail between my legs, I returned home to my *real life* and everything I was desperately running away from. I told Jerry the whole story. I braced myself for the impact of his anger and was prepared to leave, certain I could never be forgiven. I would have to begin my life—what felt left of it anyway—on my own.

Scheduled to fly another trip later that afternoon, I was in the shower and began sobbing, unable to remove the ring we both wore since we'd made a commitment to one another. I don't think it hit me until then, when I realized what a huge mistake I had made and how many lives were in the crossfire. I did not want to go. *I did not want to be alone.* Jerry and I made love, both of us apologizing profusely for not being honest with each other and allowing distance to separate us without fighting back. We talked candidly, probably for the first time in our young relationship, and agreed to see a therapist together to try and save what we had already built.

▲

WEEKS LATER I tried to contact Mario to see how he was and to wish him well. His roommate answered the phone and told me Mario had to check himself into a mental health clinic and had taken a lengthy leave of absence from work. I was also told—quite sternly—to never call again. Right then I knew I'd caused an enormous explosion with shrapnel and casualties. I had to take full responsibility. I never attempted to contact Mario again. I also found a different men's room at the airport and minded my own business.

Life tosses treasures and trials in your lap, whether you're ready for them or not. I still live with the guilt of holding another human being hostage. It took time and gut-wrenching work to heal the deep wounds and regain the trust I had demolished with Jerry. And while the wounds I caused Jerry eventually healed, the scar is still visible, even though we'll soon celebrate our twenty-fifth anniversary together. I retired my wings many years ago and take *both* of my illnesses seriously; and I work hard not to hide behind either of them. I'd be lying if I said I never think of Mario and wonder how he's doing, if he's happy and well. I hope so.

JUST WALLY AND ME
ALLEN MACK

I'VE ALWAYS BEEN attracted to older men, tall, in-charge, masculine guys who are responsible, intelligent, and past the years of flightiness. Fate favored me one night some years ago when I'd gone to the *C'est Soir*, one of the many dance bars in Manhattan's West 70's, with a friend, David. I say "fate," because it happened to be at that bar, on that night, with that particular friend, that I met—if I may wax corny—"the man of my dreams." David had had a brief fling with this gorgeous hunk years earlier and introduced us.

Tall? Ah yes, a six-footer. Masculine? Even his handshake incited a tingling in my chimes. Intelligent? I became hypnotized by the glint of cleverness in his amazingly blue eyes—even in bar lights. And, while not a prerequisite, he was handsome as hell to boot. Also, he was an older man, half again as old as I was. He was twenty-seven!

Oh, well, too good to be true. I might as well forget it.

When David went off to dance, "Hunk" and I slipped into a banquette along the wall. We sat and talked and—something I'd never done before—actually held hands. I'd held lots of other things in my short-but-active career, but holding his hand seemed so much more personal. David stopped by some time later to check on us. He took one look, rolled his eyes with silent-movie subtlety, and, with a Gloria Swanson-Swan Lake fluttering of his arms, slunk back through the crowd of hip-thrusting dancers. As I watched David leave, I was gently pulled toward my new amour who introduced into me an excitement that nearly equaled an orgasm. And I do mean "into" literally, since he began exploring the interior of my right ear with his tongue. WOW! This was even better than holding hands. Lest you get the impression, due to my ever-so-tender years, that this is a "My First Time" confession of a fragile, semi-virgin—something like being semi-pregnant—I'll fill you in a bit of my history to show that I'd had considerable experience of my own.

▲

I REMEMBER "PLAYING" with my male schoolmates in the darkened auditorium in the sixth grade, while everyone else watched the educational films we'd been scheduled to attend. One of the boys was obviously enjoying it as much as I and suggested we continue at his vacant home after school. "After school" continued for about ten years of occasional get-togethers; all it took was a certain nod or look we'd exchange when we were among the "regular" guys to determine that "game time" was definitely afoot, just enough of a prod to stiffen our resolve to get together as soon as possible.

One Sunday at church, my fourteen-year-old libido was stoked into horny tumescence, my thoughts worlds away from the mundane platitudes emanating from the podium. Times Square! The movie theaters—about which every New York City boy was warned: *They're filled with perverts*—were only a half-hour away. I tried to put the thought from my mind—while I counted out the money for the subway token.

Broadway intersects with 42nd Street at the heart of Times Square and, looking west, I counted about a dozen theaters on both sides of the street. I walked the length, studying the marquees. The films ranged from sleazy to first-run, but which of the theatres had what I was really looking for? Finally, I decided on a movie I wanted to see anyway. If other things didn't work out, at least I'd have seen a good picture. I chose *The Egyptian* with Edmund Purdom, due to a fascination with ancient history—I'd loved the book and I was rarely without one—so what had I to lose?

It was early on a Sunday afternoon and the theater was only about a quarter full. The occupied seats were widely spread out. I took a seat in the center of the orchestra about halfway down toward the screen; the rest of the aisle was empty. I couldn't have been there five minutes before a man began making his way toward me from the right aisle. He was carrying a topcoat—it was August. He sat beside me, accidentally draping his coat fully across my lap, which, I must admit, made me just a tad nervous. His left hand managed to swiftly cup my crotch with a gentle squeeze.

What do I do now?

I hadn't much time to ponder the situation, since I realized that another man—guess what he was carrying—was approaching me from the left aisle. He sat on the other side of me, draped his coat across the one already on my lap and immediately followed this maneuver by clumsy groping beneath and between the pre-set layers. Now I really didn't know what to do. My only thought—read fear—was that the two encroaching hands would meet on my dick, and a free-for-all snatch-and-run would create havoc. An image of Egypt's crocodile god flashed on the screen with its rows of teeth bared. Something had to be done and quick. I turned to look into Groper-Left's face—the glare from Purdom's gold skirt provided plenty of light to see clearly—and then I turned to look into Groper-Right's.

"Follow me out," I said to Groper Right, having quickly decided that he was more my type. I shed the double layer of coats and rushed up the aisle to the lobby. Groper-Right arrived within seconds; it turned out his name was Charlie and he was the nicest man. He took me to his office since his jealous lover was home—I didn't even know guys had other-guy lovers—and announced to the building security guard that I was his nephew.

Sex with an adult was great! Charlie couldn't get enough of this fourteen-year-old body. Or at least his tongue couldn't; he put it into places that I didn't know were allowed. Did everyone do these things? I reciprocated as best I could, but didn't know lots of stuff. Charlie took me to dinner and we made a date to meet at a subway station two weeks later. Last names and phone numbers were not exchanged.

I passed the next two weeks with a perpetual semi. When the day finally came, I arrived early and waited, and waited. Finally a stranger got off the train, came directly up to me and asked, "Are you waiting for Charlie?"

I nodded yes.

"I'm Harry," he told me, "Charlie's 'friend' got really upset when he told him he was going out. He asked me to meet you, if that's okay with you. He was afraid he'd lose contact otherwise. We can go to my place if you like. It's just another couple of stops."

"Okay," I told him, my dick turning in the direction he'd indicated, like a divining rod. Off I went for another great sex session, this time with a new face and in an actual bed!

I played with each guy off and on for years. As time passed, the sex was discarded but the friendships endured forever; through them I met many other gays, occasionally ending with sex, more often with friendship. When I became "legal" at eighteen, I decided to check out the gay bars; I went every weekend, mainly to dance. Drinks and tricks were secondary. Life was fun. The sex was casual, of little importance other than to enjoy it and get to know other people, some more intimately than others. I was having a wonderful time and the last thing in the world I wanted was to tie myself down with a lover, or any other sort of commitment.

▲

WHEN I MET Wally at the *C'est Soir*—oh, I hadn't mentioned his name before, had I? I was so caught up in Wally's eyes when David was introducing us that I hadn't heard a word he'd said, even his name. Which turned out to be awkward, masking my lack of knowledge with ah's and uh's, and calling him "handsome" whenever I couldn't cover with anything else.

"My name is Wally," he finally said, with a grin. "I was wondering how long you'd try to fake it without asking."

I just smiled my most boyish smile.

We spent the night and the next day together and, wonder of wonders, things got even better. He was hairy. I love hair on a man—that sounds dumb, doesn't it? I certainly wouldn't like to see it on a child.

We discovered problems with the time we could spend together. I worked a normal forty-hour-week. He was a singer in a Broadway musical and worked evenings and matinees at the theatre, leaving only Sundays, just one full day a week for Wally and me. He also had a roommate, who didn't seem too fond of me. He wanted the apartment to himself when Wally was working, so I had to find a way to pass the hours away from home.

We spent much time apart, while our feelings for each other drew us closer. One afternoon I rode the subway with him to the theater district, planning to continue to my parents' home for the evening. As he rose to exit the car, he leaned toward me and whispered, "I love you."

My throat constricted; my eyes filled and my hands trembled—another first in my life. He stood beyond the car windows with a great smile on his face and waved as I was swept away into the darkness of the tunnel toward the next stop.

I lived with my parents, but Wally and I continued to meet until the lease he shared with his roommate expired. Then a new apartment would be ours. When the day finally came, we were ecstatic. Leaving my parents' wasn't a big deal. I'd been spending so much time away, I wasn't sure they'd even notice. It wasn't until years later that my mother told me they didn't think I'd last a month on my own. They didn't learn about Wally until much later.

We'd been settled in about a year—newlyweds, honeymooners—when we learned about the breakup of a long-term couple, close friends of ours. One had "cheated" on the other and jealousy roused the "victim's" rage to near-homicidal levels. Everyone knew that the other partner had been "cheating" for years, but that seemed to make no difference. We, of course, were horrified, but suddenly realized that we weren't immune to such a situation. It was time for serious discussions, decisions and agreements. Early on, Wally had said, "I want a relationship, not an affair." At the time I wasn't quite sure that such a commitment was right for me, but said that I agreed.

We had both played around quite a bit through our lives and, admittedly, enjoyed it. Once we committed to each other, however, we were strictly monogamous. At eighteen, I'd been out longer sexually than Wally had, so I was no innocent. Sex with other people was merely a diversion, certainly an expression of love, but not love itself by our reasoning. We couldn't understand the melodrama some couples went through after discovering that their "other half" had screwed around.

We knew when Wally's show closed on Broadway, he might have to "go out of town" for weeks, even months. I'd taken a time consuming job in the travel field, which required jaunts to various parts of the world. Neither of us expected the other would or should remain celibate during the extended periods we spent apart. We agreed it would be acceptable to "fuck around" during such times when either one of us was out of town.

However, there had to be some ground rules, not written down or sworn before a judge, but out of respect for each other:

1) Neither of us was to play with anyone else more than once. Repetition led to outside attachments, unbidden, unwanted, but destructive.

2) Neither of us was to encroach on the time spent with the other when we were in   the same location. When we went

somewhere together, we returned home together. No outside "dates," staying overnight elsewhere, etc.

Some said that such an arrangement meant we didn't love each other. We just laughed at that nonsense, knowing so many of the "holier than thou" banner wavers secretively went off to play more often than most. Outside sex was, to us, simply an adventure, not affection. But that was just us.

Our arrangement worked perfectly, even enabling us to talk and joke about "encounters" we'd had, some even leading to occasional, very satisfactory threesomes—frivolous pastimes as long as Party #3 didn't favor just one of us.

Except on one occasion when I returned home from work to discover that Wally had a guest—cute, if you like twinks, which I don't at the best of times—friendly—if you ignore the limp handshake. And curiously, he was emptying items from an open suitcase that didn't belong to us. *Oh?* my raised eyebrows conveyed to Wally, who looked about to faint. Not receiving a reply, I motioned for him to follow me from the living room toward the bedroom. The double bed was greatly mussed due, I guessed, to some heavy-duty screwing. They had fucked in MY BED while I was at work.

"What," I said, keeping my balled fists at my sides, "is going on? Who is that?"

"He just showed up this morning. I knew him when we played in Cleveland. I didn't know he was coming, I swear!"

"And is he planning to live here? He seems to have brought an entire trousseau with him."

"I don't know what he's planning. I hardly know him."

"You're not going to tell me that he got this romantic 'elopement' into his head after a single fuck session, are you? What was he, your steady hump for the whole out-of-town-tryout?"

There was dead silence, and then he nodded. "Pretty much, yes. But I never meant to lead him on. I told him about you, that we were a permanent couple."

Wally never lies. He told me this when I accused him of lying about something many years ago. I was dubious at first. Everyone lies. My friend Harry once said that gays are born liars. "We have to be, it's called self-preservation." And back then, it was true. But through the years I realized that Wally always told the truth even if it hurt.

"So the entire cast you introduced me to when I joined you that weekend knew you were screwing around behind my back. I guess some of them got a big laugh out of it. I noticed that a few seemed a bit awkward when we met, and I wondered why. And you managed to spend my working hours fucking in MY BED?"

"I don't know what to say."

"He must be pretty stupid to follow you all the way here without being asked."

He must be pretty stupid? What the hell does that make me? I'm talking calmly and rationally while my life is being torn apart. I should be busting heads.

"What do you want me to do?" Wally asked.

Obviously, my ingénue gig was over. Time to play top for a change.

"What do I want? Well, sweetheart, you caused this mess. I'm backing off and letting you handle it on your own. However, you have only two options: One, he leaves my apartment, now, alone, through the door. Or, two, you leave through the fucking window! So get working on it. *Now!*"

And thus ends my saga of The Other Man (twink), who was never seen or heard from again. Our rules still stand and will continue to do so, just Wally and me.

History has not, nor will it ever repeat itself in my home, bet on it.

And for those who smugly reiterate, "arrangements" or "open relationships can't work," just step back and look closer at what we have. Last month we celebrated the fifty-fifth anniversary of our meeting, and this month, four years of a legal marriage in San Diego.

Our lifestyle can't work for everyone, of course, but, hey, what does?

WAY OFF
DAVID PRATT

FOUR YEARS INTO our relationship, I knocked the plug of Rob's answering machine out of the wall. I stuck it back and ran off, dimly aware that…didn't the machine need to be reset or…something?

That evening on the phone his voice was low and cold. "You have never supported my career, and this fucking well shows it." I could see the sweat on his lip. We spent the next two nights apart.

Rob was an actor. Sometimes. That is, in his core, as he defined himself, he was always and forever an actor. But by any objective measure, he was hardly one at all. During our time together, he would announce to friends, "I've quit the business" or "I'm back in the business," and either way, it would be news to me. Once, he reinforced his return to "the business," by changing his bank PIN to "ACTOR."

So the morning I messed up his answering machine was the very morning that an agent or a casting director *might* have called to offer the audition of a lifetime, which *might* have turned into the job of a lifetime, which *might* have led to the career Rob always wanted. But, unable to leave a message, they would go to the next name on their list.

In reality, such people rarely called Rob. Now near forty, Rob had not had a paying acting job in more than ten years, except for a bit as a hotel clerk in a soap opera. Yet for two nights he chose to sleep with an illusion, rather than with me. Because the reality that ruled his life—that ruled *our* life—was that an agent or casting director always *might* call with an audition, which *might* turn into a job, which *might* lead to more jobs, which *might* finally start his career. But it never happened. Rob took scene classes and motivational seminars. He dropped out of the business. He went back into the business. The phone stayed silent. So, often, did he.

So there I sat with my own silent phone in my Times Square apartment, facing a night without Rob's warm, broad body.

But let's not mope. Let's have some fun. We're on Times Square. Let me show you my neighborhood at my favorite time of day. Once you have gone through it—and beyond—you will understand how Rob endured that limbo all those years, and you will understand what led him, in the course of his decade with me, into physical relationships with two other men, and, perhaps more important, emotional ones with countless other blurred and conflated stars of his imagination, who obscured and stood in for the great goddess, Art.

So come with me through the looking glass...

Seven-thirty on a spring evening. The peach-colored sunset over the Hudson shades into blue between the midtown skyscrapers. A few stars are visible. Suitors clutching tickets come to meet their beloveds. Pastel tourists hurry from Olive Garden; businessmen stride from neon tapas bars; acting students hover with standing room tickets. The setting sun surrenders the day to flashing marquees. Up above, behind warm, grimy windows, shadowy others move and chat, apply rouge and eyeliner, sing scales, sip tea with honey and lemon. Soon these silhouettes will step into three shining dimensions, radiate their divine gifts and thus answer the dreams, desires, longings, maybe also the hatreds and frustrations of their audiences. They are containers, vehicles; they are screens on which we project our ancient rage, a situation that doubles in complexity if we want to be them.

Rob and I sat in those audiences. Across the dim, radiant space we measured ourselves against other men chosen for that timeless paradise of the stage, men the world loved and valued as it had not loved or valued us, men who had a duty denied us: that of redeeming others. Rob still dreamed of being up there in that paradise. Didn't he? Or did he just not know how to tell us that he had let go?

I had let the dream go quietly and early, before graduating college. I regretted it, I suppose, but I could bear regret; by then it was my constant companion. What I could not bear was the humiliation and invalidation to which I would be subjected if I got up on a stage outside the forgiving cocoon of college theater. Rob, however, thrived on humiliation. He could turn any remark or incident against himself, and so he wedded himself to this bizarre profession, with its twelve percent employment rate, in which his face and body and abilities and sexuality and even his soul would be coin. Escaping an abusive childhood, he had majored in theater back in Texas and then come to New York in the 1970's. He studied with Uta Hagen. He came out and began a series of codependent relationships with other actors messed up on drugs, alcohol, other men, on the acting profession itself. Acting is the ideal and the worst profession for a gay man, allowing, yea, forcing him to reenact rejection and self-doubt day after day. A high school tour put on by the Hartford Stage Company allowed Rob to join Actors Equity in 1978. Hartford Stage was to be his first and last union theatre job.

So, was Rob an actor?

He was an actor, as I am now a writer, because, in the arts, we allow love of the art and mere desire to be an artist to confer identity, regardless of achievement. You wouldn't guess this from the shame attached to lack of achievement, shame so unbearable that arts people will use any verbal ruse to create the impression that they are working and earning money at their art.

To see this better, let us leave the lights of Broadway. Let us turn a corner to a dark, uncertain place, where thousands of suitors like Rob go nightly to find beloveds: West Thirty-Sixth Street or West Fifty-Fourth, over by Ninth or Tenth Avenue. The crowds thin. Beggars stand in doorways. We locate the narrow, unnamed building, press the intercom button, and the speaker crackles. The door buzzes, we pull, we push. Inside we mount creaking stairs. On the fourth floor we stand with the actors' friends and family. A young man parts a black curtain. We fill half the seats of the tiny space, if that. Still, we can't help but be hopeful. One always is before a stage. Or on one.

This is where Rob and I met. In 1981, Rob's straight pal Fred produced and starred in two short plays by one Jeffrey Essman, in a tiny space on Forty-Seventh and Tenth. I was the stage manager. Rob, who had acted with Fred in Hartford, sat out front with the gray money box and tore tickets from a big spool that never shrank. We checked each other out. One night, reviewing our coordination of house and lobby lights, he laid a large, warm hand on my forearm. I reciprocated. Closing night we went for burgers, then to have sex at his place.

For Fred, the one-acts were only the beginning. Fred *really* wanted to mount an off-Broadway production of Essman's full-length *The Street Tonight*, which he called *The Street*. "When I do *The Street*," he would say, or "This reminds me of an incredible scene in *The Street*." When he spoke of *The Street* he thrust out his chest and placed his legs apart. *The Street* had guns and booze, and the characters said "fuck" a lot. I subsequently met more out-of-work straight actors who wanted to produce swaggering plays like Essman's. It would save them from the awful double fate of failing at what was a "sissy" profession to go into in the first place.

Now, as we duck through the black curtain into the world where Rob and I met—what are we here for?

We are here to see a "showcase." Equity allows the producers, often the actors themselves, to pay nothing, because these productions *showcase* the cast, attracting the attention of agents and casting directors. If such professionals do attend, they receive packets with the actors' pictures and résumés. The next day they will call and offer them auditions for Broadway or TV or movies. That is, they *might* call. Mostly they do not. Often they do not even come to the show. Many such gatekeepers said they would attend the Essman one-acts, but just two showed up in four weeks.

This showcase will probably not be good, but its cast will *feel* good. At the curtain call, the lights will come up and the cast will bow like the casts of *Wicked* or *Jersey Boys*. Friends will gush, and the actors will feel as high as Nathan Lane or Bernadette Peters. To them, this is as good as any Broadway hit, maybe more, because, you know, it is *unbelievable* how they put that *TV actor* in *Chicago*; all producers care about are *tourists*; and why is Patti LuPone supposed to be God's gift when she can't fucking annunciate? My friend Kara did Mrs. Lovett in Washington and she was *brilliant*! Acted circles around LuPone!

Rob held forth like this. He dismissed performances I liked. An actor I admired would turn out to have done a showcase with him years ago, and he would be a *complete* asshole. Conversely, actors of an older generation, Irene Worth, say, or Eva Le Gallienne, were all "brilliant."

I should mention that there are good showcases, some very good, that make careers or transfer to commercial runs. But, given the insane calculus of time (little) and money (less), most showcases turn out poorly. Actors do them year after year to "practice their craft," or maybe just to stay busy because to abandon art, to exit the timeless world of creation, feels like castration and death.

What, precisely, are they thinking?

Do they think stardom is just around the corner? Are they so practical as to envision so-so careers that will still be better than most: a month at a regional theater, unemployment, a temp job, a commercial, a regional again? First Footman in Hartford. Thane of Ross in Milwaukee. Do they just want to extend that college world of late night rehearsals and suitemates in the front row? Rob had a more morally charged vision: He was *destined* to be an actor. If you challenged his destiny or any step he took (or not) to fulfill it, you spent the night alone. While he clung to Art. Or to another man.

What *do* the Robs of this world think?

They do not think. They are in love. Bitterly, disappointedly, frustratedly, ambivalently, deeply in love. In high school, in college, their lover promised so much. They wedded her. Then, in the canyons of New York, she became moody, changeable, traitorous, abusive. Still, some do stick with her no matter how many times they are abandoned or betrayed. There remains that warm glow at the end of the night—on those nights she deigns to spend with them. So they take from "the business" what they would never take from another person. Or maybe they would take it from another person, which would explain why they take it, eagerly, from "the business."

It can only mean trouble to intrude upon an actor's love for the stage. From the start, you are the other man, and your adoration can never compensate for the stage's abuse. Your failures will be conflated with the abuses of "the business," in this universe where desire pumps in your lover's veins, where he inhales desire, exhales it, then inhales it again as quickly as possible for fear of losing it.

Lest I appear to blame Rob's frustrated theatre obsession for my own unhappiness, let me tell you about my relationship with the theater. In high school and college, I, like Rob, lived for the theatre. I appeared in every play. I worked in my high school theatre weekends and vacations, and in college I acted, directed, hung lights, and built and painted sets. I grew up in the fecund Connecticut River Valley, attending the private school where my parents worked. The theater was a barn-style building smelling of old wood and dust and makeup. From the doors where we loaded scenery, I looked out over the Farmington River flood plain. We were smart and funny and eccentric. There were rivalries and cliques, but we were too few, too close, too busy and too well brought up to be brutal. We were one another's lovers, but without sex. We did not share blood, but we shared a vision. Not a vision of stardom—few of us went on in theater—but of a way life should be, all art and laughter and singing and the call of, "Half hour!" Half hour 'til messed-up little me would show them all.

I did love the art itself, the thrill of a thing created. And that thrill fed the giddy fun of our in-jokes and comic bits and the beauty of the spring fields around us, just as our cleverness and bits and talking in accents fed the energy with which we went at Shakespeare, Brecht and, yes, Shepard.

Rob loved the art, too. The thoughtfulness of dissecting the playwright's warm impulse, the ecstasy of embodying it. I don't know if he had a river valley or a barn, but he had to have something. The way the night smelled going home after a performance. The exaltation and the sense of importance that detonated his desire, but safely, in the company of others like him. Then he graduated into barrenness. On the hard streets of New York, how could he get that exaltation and importance back? By auditioning of course, and taking classes, and sharing the frustrations with others similarly affected over beers at McHale's, a bar, long demolished now, on the corner of Forty-Sixth and Eighth. He could also regain the exaltation, or so he thought, by taking me, a lover so much younger. And when I disappointed him, the exaltation and the pain could be reignited with other men, who possessed what it turned out I lacked.

I could not bring myself to pursue acting professionally. Onstage I felt anxious and unfocused. Who was up there in my overweight and awkward body? Worst of all, could I ever play roles in which I was supposed to love a woman?

I retreated into vague dreams of directing, but being a self-starter scared me more, so I decided that first, as preparation, I should gain experience as a stage manager, the one who runs the actual performance, a career that can prep you for directing, but in which I had no actual interest. I stage-managed a few shows, way off Broadway, one of them being the Essman one-acts that introduced me to Rob. I was twenty-four. He was thirty-five, an age at which many actors reassess their lives and leave "the business." He laid his hand on my forearm. He was kind and safe and as frightened of success as I was. In spite of his painful self-sabotage in "the business" and his codependence and befuddlement in the rest of life, he could be a commanding top or a vigorous equal. It was the one time he knew what he wanted. We went to movies together, walking late on summer evenings to the nearby sixplex. Like me, he became excited over artful obscurities like *Man Facing Southeast* and *La Nuit de Varennes*. We stood in the freezing cold to get into *Sophie's Choice* on my twenty-fifth birthday. We shared a vision of how life should be, except that Rob already resented that it was not that way and maybe never would be. I had feared that was true for some time, but I had hope. Hope that could not be realized if I stayed with him. Which I did. So it wasn't.

Next, I spent some years as dramaturg to a fledgling theater company. I read scripts sent to us and typed up my thoughts; I could appear to be doing something while letting others handle the big, scary tasks of starting a theater in New York. By the time of my exile for not resetting the answering machine, I had retreated further. I had quit the theatre company and begun writing fiction, an even more private activity. A writer can go for years without producing results. And I did. And no one questioned me, because art is a high and private calling. No one dares say, "Nothing happening? Shouldn't you maybe do something else?"

We are back in my apartment, back from our tour of the Theater District. So let us ask how I spent those two nights exiled from Rob's bed. I wrote fiction now; did I spend those nights working on the Great American Novel?

No.

I went to see other men.

I stripped, dressed in rugby shorts and a tank top, and headed out past Broadway theaters where I would never appear, running headlong for a different kind of showcase in the narrow peep show booths of Times Square, where I watched gay porn and sometimes "performed" through a little window for the guy in the next booth. Alongside the abandoned theaters of Forty-Second Street, far from the hits of Broadway, I found, in porn, the idea of the other man in its most concentrated form. I'd catch a guy's eye, we'd slip into side-by-side booths, drop quarters, and his eye would appear at the crotch-level window. I'd strip. After a few seconds his eye would withdraw and I'd hear him leave the booth. If porn booths offer concentrated otherness and manliness, they also offer concentrated rejection, making them perfect theaters for enacting the long-running drama *I'm Not Good Enough*. You see why I wasn't succeeding as an artist. I was busy with other men, finally bringing them back to the midtown retreat maintained for the creation of my fiction.

But what of Rob's other men?

The first of them, Leland, was the real affair—real sex, real pain for me.

Leland came about because of a "scene night."

Scene nights are showcases comprising unrelated scenes, chosen by the actors to showcase their abilities and get work from industry people who (might) attend. Our first summer together, Rob appeared in two scene nights. I forget the first but vividly remember the second. Rob's scene, from a lesser Neil Simon play called *Star-Spangled Girl*, was painful self-sabotage, an enactment of his worst fears about himself. The pace was halting, energy low, characters ill-defined, lines shaky. Rob and his scene partner seemed to have no idea why they were there. They just had to do something, had to believe they were "putting themselves out there," keeping hope on a respirator.

After, I went out with Rob and the other actors. As I walked ahead, they shredded an actress they knew who had recently—*unbelievably*—gotten a job at the Hartford Stage. Rob's voice got louder and bitchier as he described a dreadful past performance by this person. Did he have any idea what I had just seen? I think so. I think they all did. That is why the conversation rose to such a pitch. They were self-medicating, as I self-medicated in peep shows. Their bitching made them feel better, but it infuriated me, partly because I had my own theater issues, partly because I was not allowed to speak. Even now, thirty years later, I tremble to type what I wanted to say then: "Guys, are you aware of the quality of your own performances tonight?" I just did not say it. Their dedication to art made them unassailable.

The bitching continued over drinks. I was twenty-six and sitting with people in their thirties and forties carrying on about how agent X was "a cunt" and actor Y a "joke" who got certain roles only because...I grew angry and quiet. It became an uncomfortable evening, which led to a more uncomfortable ride home. Finally I had to say it: I resented sitting through something that was, well, not very good, then having to swallow how awful some actress was who had just gotten an actual job at the Hartford Stage.

Rob did not take my confession well. In the morning, when I kissed him good-bye, he did not open his eyes or speak.

In August, he planned a trip back to Texas. The Sunday before he left, we visited my friend Lorie in Brooklyn. It was important that Rob leave by a certain time, in order to have cappuccino with "a friend" in Manhattan.

This cappuccino was with Leland, as was the sex that followed. Leland had been stage manager of the scene night. The scene had failed, no agents had come, no casting directors called, so Rob went to Heaven with Leland.

"I'm seeing another man."

His revelation was touching, on a park bench in Brooklyn, a September Sunday, the first whiff of autumn in the air. He said it did not affect how he felt about me. (He did not ask if it affected how I felt about him.) We were not breaking up, he promised. We had just come to such an impasse, things had become so heavy, and Leland was so open and playful...We went back to my apartment and of course made love. The affair with Leland brought us closer. And I was smashing in the role of The Injured Party at Rob's Railroad Apartment Theater. It is a fun and satisfying role when you think you have a lock on the one injuring you. Your easygoing acceptance of the situation can impress him and make him feel bad. I could enjoy being "mature" and "sophisticated" about it, while not having to hurt too much and spend only certain nights alone. I smugly enjoyed the fact that Leland would not take it up the ass from Rob, while I would. I smugly enjoyed the fact that Rob shared this with me.

Eventually Leland gave Rob the heave-ho, pointedly ignoring him through an entire evening with friends. I got what I wanted. Or what I thought I wanted. I did not see the affair as an opportunity to leave a relationship that was not working. I saw it as a challenge to prove I was good enough. I did not feel triumphant or relieved when I "won" Rob back. By the time Leland was over Rob, I was over the whole thing. I "won" nothing. I was the default. Back to being the other man in relation to "the business." So what had Leland been? The *other* other man? Did he embody "the business" for Rob? Did sex with the stage manager somehow mean, in Rob's mind, success in the business? No agents came to get him off, so…Later I learned that there are some men and women, straight and gay, who sleep their way through showcase after showcase, often identifying the sexual opportunities before accepting roles or putting together companies. Fortunately, this was not Rob.

Next was Trent, the other man Rob did not have sex with. The straight one. The nineteen-year-old one.

As Rob went in and out of "the business," Trent turned up as a temp in the theater ticket office where Rob worked. Such seasonal jobs comprise, for actors, a whole universe parallel to that of fourth-floor walk-up theaters on Tenth Avenue.

Rob was by then almost forty. Legions of his peers had quit "the business." Trent, as I said, was nineteen, just arrived in New York from Indiana. He left the office almost every day to audition for the new Eddie Murphy or Sigourney Weaver or Nic Cage movie. Trent voiced his anxieties over these auditions to the entire office, but mostly to Rob, who sat next to him. Trent may not have fully understood the emotional buttons he hit in Rob, but he knew he hit them. He also knew he was hot, as when he complained to Rob thus: "I'm tired of them asking me to take my shirt off!" Trent was getting a lot of attention from an older man. Who at nineteen doesn't lap that up? And Rob was a comforting presence. He hurried over when Trent had to unburden himself over the loss of a girlfriend or a role. (Just which roles Trent was up for, I do not know. Rob believed he stood on the edge of stardom, but he may have been auditioning for "Second Man" or "Guy in Rabbit Costume.")

Like many artists and performers, Rob had a fascination with the healing arts. He taught yoga to Trent and gave Trent reiki. Nude. One morning, with a quickening of my heart, I found in Rob's dresser a cache of lubricant, condoms, latex gloves, Polaroid film, and a camera. No, really. When you recount these things they sound ridiculous. Do people really *do* that stuff? Yes, they do. And, on their hands and knees, already late for work, they search for the pictures taken. Rob entered. "They're under J," he said, indicating his card file—J was Trent's last initial. I pretended I had no idea what he meant. He walked away. I looked under J.

There they were: Trent in bikini underwear in various yoga poses; Trent with his shirt off doing sit-ups, face scrunched adorably. Trent from behind, naked, legs spread, arms stretched above his head, his impressive penis reflected in the mirror on the door, a stroke—pardon the expression—of luck, as Trent wouldn't let Rob shoot him from the front. Later, when I was alone, I jerked off to these pictures. I cajoled Rob for details. He told me everything, including how he inserted two gloved and lubed fingers up Trent's rectum in the course of a massage. I suggested ways for Rob to get Trent to go further. I hoped for more pictures. I hinted for a threesome. Trent was nonthreatening. Rob would never have him.

Still I could nurse a little hurt. I would never look like that. I would never be that young again. As Rob closed in on forty, I closed in on thirty. And even when I was young, I was not like Trent. I never had promise. No one had wanted me the way Rob and so many in "the business" wanted Trent. Trent was Rob's and my impossible dream of ourselves, the resurrection of a hoped-for self that had died and had not been properly mourned. We longed to incorporate Trent—or a young man very much like him but yet unseen and just out of reach—into ourselves and be whole. Then the lights would shine on us. Then the audience would rise, and at last we would be who we were meant to be.

Trent and Rob "broke up," as it were, slowly. Rob tired of holding Trent's hand through break-ups and make-ups with the girlfriend. He tired of hearing about the cruelties of "the business." He and Rob both left the ticket office. Rob became a dresser on Broadway, caring for the costumes of the men he wanted to be, coming home angry and exhausted, steps leaden on the stairs. I pretended to be asleep.

"The business" ultimately was not so good to Trent. IMDB lists a handful of roles over the years—"Frank," "Vince," "Office Assistant," "Cop #1"—and a picture of him, still handsome in his forties. His last few jobs have been voice-overs. He is divorced. Three kids. None of this is to say he is not happy. None of this is to say being Cop #1 is not important, or that Trent does not experience a high, a glimpse of stars in a royal blue sky, when he thinks of his next role.

For Rob, IMDB has one credit, a role in a short film in 1998. There is no picture, there is no date of birth, nor is there…well, I won't get ahead of myself.

As Rob and I approached the decade mark, I more and more sought my own Trents on-screen in Eighth Avenue peep shows, and sometimes in person. Needing to heighten the experience, I began bringing guys back to my Forty-Ninth Street apartment. Some were sweet and smart and eager to please and be pleased, but I never saw any of them again. I never took a phone number. If they wanted to do more than get naked and jerk off, I told them, "I'm protecting someone." Indeed I was. In more ways than one. Rob didn't know. Not consciously, anyway.

One night, a young man from Massachusetts demanded ten dollars. I negotiated him down to two and a token.

A guy smoked crack in my apartment, and, once I got him out, I quit going to peep shows for several weeks. Then I forgot how scary it was: the guy high, angry, refusing to leave, and I went again.

Rob and I broke up when two things happened: (1) A guy I brought home robbed and threatened me, pushing me into a recovery group for sexual compulsion; and (2) I began publishing short stories. Rob insisted on buying his own personal copy of the magazine that carried my first story, but no matter how carefully I explained its location on the rack at Coliseum Books, he couldn't find it. Same with my second story. My twelve-stepping proceeded. I had no more other men. Neither did he. We had each other less and less. By the end of 1992 the relationship had run its course, and I moved permanently into the Forty-Ninth Street apartment. A few weeks later, Rob brought two bags of my belongings to the Times Square apartment, where I now lived full time. We chatted briefly. He left. I closed the door, and I cried about the breakup for the first and only time. I did feel sad and lonely and afraid, but what I mostly felt was relieved. I remodeled the apartment. I joined a gay writing workshop. Eventually I dated and slept with other guys.

A few years later, I heard that Rob had been cast in a Bruce Willis film. But his mother fell ill, and he had to withdraw to go to her in Texas. Then, in the early 2000's, he developed a brain tumor. We were not in communication then; I heard about it through friends. He stabilized and hung on a few years, visiting friends and relatives around the country who were in the midst of similar health crises. He helped and comforted them. I got the impression that at last he had found his true work. Then the tumor returned, and he had to stop. He gave up his New York apartment and returned to Texas. His condition worsened. I was told that he believed he was going to appear in a film of *Les Misérables*.

In January 2005 I received two long messages on my answering machine. Rob greeted me expansively. His voice was vigorous and excited as I had never heard it. He was better, he said, and back in New York, beginning work on "the movie" a few blocks from my apartment. He did not speak explicitly of forgiveness or reconciliation, but these were the subtext.

I called a mutual friend. Was Rob indeed better? Was he here? I knew he wasn't making *Les Misérables*, but could it be that he was making something?

No.

He was in Texas, in the hospital.

Two weeks later, he died.

Times Square is now "cleaned up." Along Eighth Avenue and Forty-Second Street, tourists in pastels crowd into chain restaurants and Sephora and Madame Tussaud's. The city and the theatre owners, including newer, more corporate ones, have rehabilitated the old legit theaters: Disney's *Mary Poppins* at the New Amsterdam; *Spider-Man* across the street at the Foxwoods. High-flyers, adored. And to dozens of tiny theaters down the side streets, those with feet made a bit more of clay troop every night, hoping for a little adoration they can call their own. They and their audiences are the lifeblood of the city, even if their obsession is misguided or their vision unrealistic, even if they are caught in abusive affairs or rage about TV stars in *Chicago*. They fell in love one night during an eighth-grade *Camelot*. They followed their love here and kissed in the moment between day and night when shadows above the marquees sang scales and prepared to greet a thousand suitors. We may not know their names, but we need them. The city needs them. Their suffering and their joys *make* New York City, just as much as the stars and audiences of *Mary Poppins*.

The clay-footed ones in the tiny theatres even have a patron saint. He is Fred, Rob's friend who wanted to star in Jeffrey Essman's *The Street Tonight*.

In late 1982, I and some friends founded one of those tiny theater companies. I told you about this; I was the dramaturg. I was young and wanted to impress my colleagues. Well, I knew someone who knew Jeffrey Essman. I called Fred and arranged a meeting. Essman was fine with Fred doing a reading of *The Street* with us. It was all set. Then late one night Essman called me. (Me!) He had been thinking and thinking and felt terrible and didn't know what to do, but, well, Fred, who was past thirty-five now, was just too old for *The Street*.

"These are kids!" Essman said of his beer-swilling ne'er-do-wells who said fuck a lot. He promised not to involve me in the humiliation he should have headed off. He wrote Fred a letter. Fred learned from a letter that he had lost forever the show he had dreamed of, counted on, and talked about for years. Our reading of The *Street Tonight* ultimately featured a rising twenty-something who had the night off from his Broadway show; it was listed in the *Times* and was packed, though our little company failed before we could mount a full production.

I never spoke to Fred again.

But I saw him.

At the time of the one-acts, Fred waited tables at Conjunto's, a burger place on Seventh Avenue South. In later years I passed Conjunto's and saw Fred, still reciting specials, weaving with trays, directing younger waiters with piercings, bleached hair, and dreams of their own. Then I moved uptown and for a while didn't see him. One evening, though, as the sunset shaded into blue between midtown skyscrapers, as tourists and businessmen and students gathered under flashing marquees, as silhouettes passed above, painting their faces and singing scales, down on Seventh Avenue South I passed Conjunto's and saw Fred, hair silver now, face lined. He stood before a seated party, gesturing and reciting specials. There he was: the patron saint of the theater's spurned lovers, just where he should be. He had the power to release us from all the failed projects and blown auditions, from bondage to the other men we wish we could have had or could have been, from all the other men we still wish we could be.

If I follow St. Fred, I will gain a greater reward than applause. I will gain Heaven at last. There, I will be whole. There, I will not envy or desire or regret. There, no man will be other than me. There Rob and I will embrace, once, briefly, and nothing will need to be said.

A Pitiless Love
Perry Brass

WHEN I THINK back on it, the story of how I met Morris Hart-man—the name I'll give him—seems both a revelation to me, and incredibly simple. In 1999 I published a book called *How to Survive Your Own Gay Life: An Adult Guide to Love, Sex, and Relationships.* It was my first nonfiction book, after publishing ten books of either fiction or poetry, and it came from a lifetime of being gay as well as involved with the more radical aspects of the gay movement before it became taken over by corporations and LGBT careerism. It was, in short, a book about opening up your heart and self to other men; offering a queer soup-to-nuts menu from initially meeting other guys to meeting your own deeper self and taking care of that emerging adult self in various trying situations.

I just didn't dream that I'd be in one of them.

The book was a red-hot success. My distributors and gay bookstores were crazy about it, and almost immediately, I started receiving fan letters like never before. They came from young men just coming out, and older men who had been "around that block" for years. Among the letters was a long one from an older man on the verge of coming out, who was my age exactly, fifty-one, still living with his wife and kids in one of New York's tonier suburbs. In the process of coming out, he'd been reading my fiction, even before my nonfiction book, and my work had meant "everything to him."

He finished by saying, "I'd really love to meet you, either for coffee or let me take you to dinner. My intentions are totally honorable, but it would be a great pleasure to do this."

I was intrigued, but I'd also been going through some deflating experiences with fans, and discovered that a writer's fans often find him a letdown after his books. In other words, you are not the perfect reflection of themselves that they'd found in your words, and they quickly make this evident. So I put off meeting Morris for six months. I was still promoting the nonfiction book and working on my next book; Steve, my partner of almost twenty years, and I took an enthralling river barge tour of French Burgundy. Still, during this period, I would get postcards and notes from Morris asking me not to forget him, that he really wanted to meet me.

Finally, a few weeks before Labor Day, I decided to call him. I did, and a woman answered. It was his wife; they were still living together, somewhat. "Morris is in Ireland," she told me. "Can I take a message for him?"

I left my name. Shortly after, I got a postcard from Ireland, informing me that Morris had taken his kids there. "Don't forget me, Perry," he finished.

A week before Labor Day, I called him again. This time I got an answering machine, and left a message. An hour later he called back. He was brimming with excitement that I had called. He asked me if he could take me out for dinner the Sunday of Labor Day weekend. I decided why not. I told Steve that I was going to meet a fan of *How to Survive*; he told me to be careful.

"Some of your fans have been real disappointments," he warned.

As arranged, we met on that Sunday in a restaurant in the West Village. He knew what I looked like from the back of my book covers, but I had no idea about him. I got there first, and scanned the door. Suddenly, this very attractive, compactly built man with jet-black hair and dark penetrating eyes walked in.

Dressed expensively in casual country-gentleman fashion (Harris Tweed sports jacket, pleated gray Italian wool pants), he saw me, smiled, and started talking as soon as he sat down. I quickly learned he was a highly paid, successful corporate lawyer, and in our first moments he told me how much money he made—and spent—and how expensive the suburban lifestyle he kept up was. "It cost us $7,000 a year just to plow our driveway in the winter!"

As he jabbered on, I realized he was nervous meeting me, and this rush of verbiage was obviously being used to cover up that fact; and, as he quickly revealed, he was extremely controlling and used to getting his own way. When I began to use some inroad to add something, he cut me off. "Don't interrupt me now, I've got a lot more to say."

I found myself getting bored, and asked myself was I ever going to see this man again? Finally, about an hour later, after dinner, he settled down and looked at me.

"I need to tell you something," he admitted bashfully. "When you left that message on my machine, I just played it over and over again to hear the sound of your voice."

His sharp eyes softened tenderly, and I thought: "Well..."

He had a car, and drove me back to Riverdale, in the North Bronx, where I live with Steve. Just before I got out, he asked me to sign some books of mine he had collected. There were five, he'd read all of them, and told me about them. Suddenly he leaned over and kissed me, without holding anything back. The hard lawyer part of him completely dropped off. I felt as if he had just offered me this usually withheld piece of his soul, and despite my reservations, I accepted it.

I got out, slightly off balance, and walked into my apartment. Still not sure what to do, I decided to write him a fairly formal thank you note and send it by mail. I didn't see him again for several weeks. He went to Hawaii with his three kids, and wrote me that he was moving out of his wife's house, and into an apartment of his own in another upscale suburb, in Connecticut. I invited him to a fundraiser at which I was featured reading poetry for a small musical performance organization at an arts club downtown. He showed up, and we went out to dinner afterward. Again, he couldn't wait to tell me everything about himself—just spilling it all out. I hardly said anything. But now I was definitely happy doing it. I was becoming taken with him. I wasn't even sure why—except that I felt some kind of waiting innocence being offered solely to me under his corporate lawyer shell, or was I only *inventing* this?

Since Morris, like I, had come in by commuter train, we took a cab back to Grand Central together. He told me how much the evening had meant to him, and held my hand. I smiled and went into that cloud of self-inflation you go through when someone who you feel has a ray of glamour you'd love to touch touches you. In Grand Central he walked me to my train, and kissed me good night.

Now I didn't wonder about seeing him again. There were things about him I didn't like; he definitely came from another world—a harder, closeted, straight, more monied one. But he was reaching out to me at a moment when, even without knowing it, I was wanting it—maybe even needing it. We wrote each other little notes by email, and called each other. He knew about Steve, and asked me if he ever went away for a few days. I said he did. I could feel Morris smile on the phone. I had told Steve about him, that Morris was a fan of mine, and Steve told me to watch out. As a habit, Steve who worked in health care, didn't like lawyers. "You'll find there's a lot *less* there than meets the eye," he warned.

I figured Steve was just being possessive, which he was. I had never minded it. I felt that possessiveness was simply a character trait, and there were, to me, a lot worse ones than possessiveness: like flakiness, or selfishness, or destructive ego-driven competitiveness. I had met all of these in other men, and Steve's possessiveness paled in comparison. Morris called me one afternoon a few weeks later.

"I have a great invitation for you," he announced. The Metropolitan Opera was doing a new, hugely lauded production of Richard Wagner's masterpiece of forbidden love, *Tristan and Isolde*. It was almost entirely sold out. But Morris's money-stuffed corporation had a box at the Met. "I asked for seats for this Tuesday. Would you like to go?"

I am not a total opera fan, but this production was definitely a must see. How could I refuse? There was only one hitch: Morris asked if he could spend the night in our apartment, since going back to Connecticut after a long opera would be difficult, and he had work the next day. He could drive in, park at our place, and then we'd go in together to Lincoln Center. I told Steve about it. He looked quizzical, but agreed. He had not met Morris yet, but I figured that would be inevitable.

Even after a full day of work, Morris arrived at my apartment exactly on time, looking very good. I had dressed up, and made reservations at a fairly swank restaurant near Lincoln Center. After dinner, I picked up the check. He said, "You don't have to do this, because the seats were free."

I just laughed. Since I was a few months older than Morris, I joked, "Don't question it when older men pick up the check."

The box seats were fantastic. So this is how the super-rich live? And the opera was stunning; everything that people had been saying about it was true. I was completely immersed in the production, but kept looking over at Morris. His eyes were riveted on the stage. Was he resisting the tide of emotions I was feeling? At the end, Isolde's voice soars above one of the most passionate moments in all of Western art, as she asks herself if she alone hears the melody of a love which is so all consuming, so satisfying, that it is capable of both drowning her in its intensity and yet re-creating her at the same time.

In this intensity of consummated feelings, I could have been knocked over by a feather. I kept hearing those last words sung in my head as we joined torrents of people leaving the Met, and crossed Broadway to get an express bus back to Riverdale. There I pulled out the sofa bed in the guest/TV room we have, and Morris got undressed to crawl in. I had never seen him in just underwear. He was beautiful, no doubt about it, with a very trim, still athletic body and beautiful clear skin. I couldn't keep my eyes off him, or my hands, but realized we were in a difficult situation. Steve was asleep in our room, and I was trying very hard to keep everything within bounds.

I climbed into bed with Steve, and thought: In our guest room is this man I am extremely attracted to, but, like the forbidden coupling in *Tristan and Isolde*, how is this going to end— and what can I do to *evade* all the warnings of the ending?

The next morning Steve and Morris were cordial to one another. Steve, a real opera lover, asked him about the performance. Morris was enthusiastic but didn't want Steve to feel left out, so he didn't go into any real details. Steve had to leave early for work. Morris showered after Steve left, and in a suit and tie approached me to say goodbye. I kissed him, but half a second later, he had all my clothes off and most of his own.

"I want to *submit* myself to you," he confessed. "I'm a submissive person."

He licked my feet and legs, then ventured up to my groin. I was trembling, turned on to the hilt, point-blank inside with desire for him.

He glanced at his watch. "I've got to go," he announced, jumping back into his suit. "I have an appointment at ten." He became a different person; this driven, cold look descended on his face. "I'm a lawyer," he said. "I've got to do this. You'll see, the closer I get to my office, the harder and more directed I become."

I thought, what a fast transition, but only said goodbye to him. After he was gone, I knew I had to spend more time with him. There was no way around it. It was like he had taken something totally intimate from me, and I couldn't get it back. He called me a couple of hours later from work in Stamford, apologizing. "I'm sorry I ran off. I can't talk for long, but I like what we did."

I didn't see him for the next several weeks. He was either flying around to corporate meetings, or seeing his kids. It was getting close to Christmas. We managed to have dinner together in the Village again. There he told me more about himself, about coming from a strict, striving, mother-dominated, Irish Catholic family in upstate New York, where the idea of not marrying and producing a "model" family wasn't even "in the picture" for him.

I listened sympathetically, then he told me he'd been dating someone else—an older man, in his early sixties, who was a well-known painter, named Joshua. They had met at an S & M get-together. "I've told you I'm submissive," Morris said. "Joshua's perfect for me. He's a real Master. But I don't know what to do about you. If this thing with Joshua works out, I can't see you anymore. But if Joshua will allow it, I would very much like to have a *parallel* relationship with you."

"But you hardly know him," I protested. "You're going to let him dictate this for you *already?*"

"I really want this to work out," Morris said, reverting to a coy passivity. "But I can only see you if he'll allow it."

Strangely enough, I knew Joshua. We were not friends, but nodding acquaintances from various art scenes in New York. I informed Morris that, at this point, I was *sure* Joshua wouldn't mind it if he saw me—was I merely grabbing stupidly at straws?—but it seemed that by making this kind of extreme demand so fast on Morris, Joshua would only destroy things.

"That might be true," Morris said, thinking it over seriously, again "submitting" to me. I went home and called two friends of mine who were very involved in S & M. What should I do to reach Morris? Should I try to completely dominate him? Or should I offer myself to him as an alternative to Joshua's dominance? "If Joshua is really good at this," one advised, "you don't stand a chance." The other offered me no help at all. He decided Morris, under his expensive lawyer suit, was completely flaky. "Stay away from him."

But I wasn't ready to do this. Morris emailed me now constantly, telling me how much he cared for me as a friend, how much he looked up to me. All I could feel was apologetic. I wasn't wealthy, or even sufficiently "leather daddy" enough to offer him the kind of dominance he might find appealing. The winter was severe, bone-freezing cold with snow and ice. A week before Christmas, Steve came down with a raging flu—high fever, nausea, weakness. I had to take care of him, and slept in the guest room to keep contagion down. He became delirious from fever. I was afraid we'd have to hospitalize him, but I was able to pull him through with constant care. I spoke to Morris. He told me that he wanted to see me again, and I asked him to wait until Steve got better.

▲

MORRIS HAD A few days off after Christmas, following when his kids came to spend time with him. We arranged I would take a train to Connecticut to stay with him overnight. It would be the first time we'd done this, and I was both excited and nervous. I told Steve that I had been offered a last minute reading in Philadelphia, and I'd be going there overnight. I packed a small bag, and arrived at the Stamford station a little after eight p.m. Morris picked me up. He was glowing seeing me.

We went back to his new "bachelor" apartment in a recent *luxe* town house development next to a yacht basin. The development had a nautical theme with ship pennants outside. His apartment was beautifully though minimally furnished, with two complete marble baths both equipped with Jacuzzis, perfect for an upscale couple. We had dinner at the yacht basin's candle lit restaurant then went back to his place. I felt like I was in this exquisite cloud of union with him, filled with flowers and tenderness. He was sweet and adoring, though slightly removed from me, I could tell, as if he were still trying to control every moment. I wanted to kiss him as soon as we got back, but he told me to wait. I waited in his "library," a den off the living room. He disappeared and a short time later returned wearing a fitted black S & M leather halter.

"It's a present I bought myself," he announced. He looked great in it; the straps accentuated his beautiful chest, and ended with a series of fitted genital pieces around his cock and balls. I felt as if he were offering himself to me as a present, as he took me into his large, dimly lit bedroom, displaying the most sumptuous bed I'd ever seen—massive antique oak from the late 1880's with early American faces and woodland scenes chiseled into the headboard, a marriage present he told me that he had insisted on retaining after his divorce. I felt as if my brain had split open, and he was now the only thing in it. We made love through most of the night. I got about four hours sleep. He was insatiable, and even when he dozed off, kept his arms locked tightly around me. He left a very pronounced small "hickey" on my neck, something that hadn't happened to me for years. We had to get up early the next morning. He had appointments and needed to drive me to the train station. He handed me a beautiful cotton robe, and we went into a small breakfast nook. He offered me some cereal and made coffee.

I was eating, when he looked at me. "We can never do this again," he said.

I stopped. "What?"

"*This* can *never* happen again. I won't let it. I won't allow it to happen. Joshua has told me I can't see you. I will not endanger my relationship with him in *any* way by seeing you."

"Then why'd you ask me here?"

He looked down, embarrassed. "I'd booked the time, Perry. It was already on my calendar, and I felt that I shouldn't waste it."

"Is that it?" I asked. I told him I needed to take a shower. He insisted on showering with me. In the bathroom I inanely offered, as if this would make a difference, "Are you sure you're ready to make a decision like this? Suppose you break up with Joshua in a few months?"

He shook his head. "I know I can't love two guys at the same time. Even when I was with my wife, I never once cheated on her. I never actually had gay sex until after I had left her." He paused and then explained, "I did a thorough financial study before we split up. I had to know if I could afford to live like this after our separation. I would not have separated from her if I had to live any differently."

On the way back to the train station, I thought about numerous men I had known who had left their wives after they realized the truth about themselves; some of them ended up in flophouse hotel rooms. It was more important to them to make that move than anything else.

It was breath-freezing cold out as I joined a crowd of commuters waiting to return to New York for another day of work. No one spoke on the train. In the dead silence I felt like I'd been kicked in the head, all the warmth had been drained from me, leaving only a savage disappointment. I remembered the hickey; how would I ever hide that from Steve? I got back home; Steve was there. He was sweet and asked me about the trip to Philadelphia. I told him it went fine, but I was tired. He noticed the hickey. I told him I was breaking out from wintry dry skin and fatigue. I decided I wanted nothing more to do with Morris. I wrote him a frigid email thanking him for the visit. "It's always nice to spend time with my fans."

He wrote me back that he was sorry about his decision, but it had been Joshua's. We were approaching New Year's Eve, the last one of the twentieth century. It was too momentous. I decided to call him. Joshua, he told me, was away on a short teaching job; he was alone. I told him I didn't want to see him. "I wish we could be friends," he said.

That didn't seem possible, but I had no idea what was going to happen next—the depth of the emotional vacuum I'd be sucked into. I stopped eating and sleeping for the next several days, telling Steve it was a mild flu and in this weather catching *anything* seemed impossible to avoid. Even breathing became difficult; I kept wondering what the hell was wrong with me. I hardly knew this man, and yet he was still taking my breath away, and not in a good way. I went to a New Year's Eve party with Steve and some friends. I felt like I was floating through it, trapped in some kind of plastic bag, without air.

I made a decision; for my own self-preservation I would see him. I called Morris, and told him that I *did* want to be friends. He was ebullient and suggested that since Joshua was still away we get together for dinner. We did soon afterwards, and pretended only to be casual friends. He talked about his work, and Joshua—how relieved Joshua was knowing that Morris would not see me again, certainly not romantically. I looked at him while he talked, and felt as if I were being detoxed, slowly.

We had a few more meetings like this. Now I could eat and breathe again. The hickey finally went away. I also realized how much anger was still inside me. The scene in Stamford kept playing over again in my mind—the way he had told me, so calculatedly, the next day, like I was merely an office temp he would no longer employ, someone to be cast aside. I realized I had been dead wrong, despite the level of "human bondage" I had let myself fall into, I could not be "friends" with this man again.

I decided I would tell him, in my apartment.

He drove in from Stamford on a sunny cold Saturday morning—we had planned actually to have brunch in the city. Steve was away, and we sat in my living room, a short distance from each other. I brought up what had happened in Stamford, what it had done to me.

"You have to understand, Perry, that I've kept all of my feelings in a deep freeze for decades. That was the only way I could survive as a husband, a lawyer, and myself. I'm only starting to understand feelings."

"Are you talking about your own, or anyone else's?"

He could not answer me. I looked at him, and told him that I *definitely* would not see him again. He looked shocked and then deflated, completely drained of any color. I still felt this horrible pain inside me but there was no way I could go on with this charade. He got up. "Can't we at least shake hands?" he asked.

I smiled. "Like I'm one of your clients? No."

I led him to the door and watched him disappear, then sat back down again, my heart beating so hard that my chest hurt. I really wanted things to change in the next several weeks, to get back to normal; I had a lot of work to do myself. I also found myself going into the famous "bargaining" Elisabeth-Kübler-Ross stage of grief. I kept wanting Morris to call me and say, "You're right. I shouldn't have let Joshua make that decision for me. We can have an *adult* relationship on our own. I see it now." I kept hoping that some other force would facilitate this change, that like in classical plays, some beneficent god would appear out of the stage machinery—the *"deus ex machina"*—and return me to that magical elation I had in those first moments of love with Morris, that arrived with the intensity of Isolde's passion. Finally, a month or so later, I came to another conclusion: I would have to be the *"deus"* for *myself*, to return *me* to my own equilibrium and positive self-feelings, but certainly with no Morris waiting for me.

Several years later, Morris, Joshua, and I redeveloped a cautious acquaintanceship, always tiptoeing around what had happened. Morris and Joshua became much more involved with Morris's submissiveness, in their own S & M relationship, until finally Morris tired of the role. They split up a little less than ten years after they met. Steve and I are still together.

WHERE ARE YOU GOING TO?
PAUL ALAN FAHEY

IN THE WINTER of 1974, fresh out of the Peace Corps, I was living alone and working in Chicago at Hull House daycare as a preschool teacher, while completing my master's degree at night. Most of my free time I spent cruising every public men's room in the vicinity for some romantic notion I had of finding my "heart's desire." I did find him—Bob, my soul mate of thirty-seven years—but that came later, after graduation from De Paul and after I'd moved back home to California. For the time being, I threw myself into the hunt for a partner with great vigor. It was the 1970's for chrissakes, and I was gay and out. The bushes in Lincoln Park were ripe for the picking and I wasn't planning on missing a meal.

I met Greg—that's not his name but what I'll call him—on one of those sweltering Chicago summer nights with not a breeze blowing and nothing but a close, sticky feeling in the air. Broadway Sam's wouldn't start hopping until ten at the earliest, so I walked over to the lake and sat on a chunk of concrete above the rocky beach. Not that I wasn't intimately acquainted with every leafy tree and bush in the park, but the lake was closer to home and became my regular cruising spot.

I wasn't there long before a slim, good-looking, black guy in a white T-shirt and cut-offs motioned to a spot next to me with a kind of "is this slab taken" gesture. I indicated it wasn't and he sat down, took off his black and white sneakers and crossed his legs lotus style. He had this cute half white, half black mustache, and as he talked I couldn't stop staring at him. God, he was gorgeous. We dispensed with the usual "who are you and what do you do" stuff right off and left the "what do you like" 'til later. He was a musician who played piano and sang in a local pop band. I thought it sounded glamorous and said so.

"I teach preschoolers in daycare," I said, but my words felt flat and dull compared to his enthusiasm for his music and the excitement expressed over the band's latest gig in Indiana. We eventually hit common ground. We both loved Stevie, Diana, and the Pointer Sisters, and we could dance all night to "Rock the Boat" by the Hues Corporation or anything disco.

We ended up in my apartment on Melrose. The bed was a mattress with a sheet and a pillow—an economy measure I'd acquired in Peace Corps days and couldn't seem to shake. Fortunately what we liked was mutual. Lots of deep, French kissing, body massage, and sucking each other's cock 'til the Bee Gees came home. Sexually, we fit together like a black and white sundae with hot fudge and lots of marshmallow cream.

The next day when I arrived home from work, Greg was sitting in the hallway, waiting, with a paper bag in his hand. "My toothbrush and razor," he said. Then he dragged a small duffle to my door and kicked it into my apartment. "I'm moving in, honey." Hip, funny, and smart. That was Greg. Did I say he was gorgeous?

For weeks, maybe months, we were inseparable, but then the romance waned. Little daily things, like living, got in the way. We grew apart, which looking back, was bound to happen when relationships are based on movie fantasies of romantic love. I think I knew early on the relationship wouldn't last, but for the time, it was great fun.

The end came one weekend in the winter of 1975. I'd recently completed my degree but had trouble landing a full time teaching position in special education. I remember it was one of the worst snowstorms of the season, and, with Greg out of town on a gig, I was lonely and decided to hit the local bars. It must have been around two in the morning when I heard the bartender give last call. People started to leave. The rest of us, the odds and ends, too tanked to move, lined the wall at the back, each of us desperate to go home with a partner. The weekend without Greg stretched ahead of me like an Antonioni movie without subtitles. I watched through glazed eyes while a few guys paired off and abandoned me, holding nothing but a warm bottle of Miller Lite.

I closed my eyes, wondered if I could sleep like this, leaning up against the wall while the bartender closed shop, turned off the lights and went home. Maybe he wouldn't notice.

An older guy, late thirties, early forties, came up to me, thrust his hand down the front of my Levis, and with his arm around my shoulder, led me out to the icy pavement, and to his car parked on a side street off North Broadway.

We were somewhere near Lincoln Park when he said he was a professor of sociology. He didn't name the university. He had one hand on the steering wheel, the other switching radio stations until he found a song he liked: Barry Manilow's "I Write the Songs."

He looked over at me and said, "That's my song, you know."

I didn't know. I thought Manilow wrote most of his own stuff. They all sounded the same, like one-note sambas. Only the titles were different. I had a good ear, sang along pretty good in the shower for chrissakes. But to Barry Manilow? Never.

"You wrote it?" I asked.

"No," he said, "I meant it's my song for now. I choose a new one when it suits me. I'm a man of many moods." And then, "That Barry sure can sing, huh, kid?"

I said something about my being a Midler man. I couldn't imagine this guy in class, lecturing on Durkheim and Karl Marx while Barry's tunes droned on in his head like white noise. I wondered what Greg would think if he could see me with this loser and listening to him prattle on about Manilow.

"My place or yours, kid?" the guy said, interrupting my thoughts. "This is getting old."

We passed the new DePaul campus off Seminary and the psycho-education clinic where I'd done most of my student teaching. *Christ, if those kids could see me now.*

I told him his place would be fine.

He reached down, grabbed my crotch, and worked it a little. "Okee-dokee, hon."

Jesus.

He turned onto Lake Shore Drive and we headed north.

I passed out, then woke some time later to heavy snow pelting the windshield. I squinted at the clock on the dash, but couldn't make my eyes focus.

"Where we going?" I asked.

"My place, kid."

I thought about my interview the following week at a small Catholic high school, looming over my head like Damocles' sword, and everything I should be doing to prepare instead of riding around with this loser, heading north to his place. Just to get off. We passed the Skokie exit and I asked him again. "Where we going?"

"My place. Madison, double yew, eye."

Shit! "Like in Madison, Wisconsin?"

"Uh-huh."

Wisconsin. I knew it was somewhere north of Chicago, but U.S. geography was never my strong suit. I hardly ever thought about it. I had visions of checkpoints, gates going up and down, and officials stamping passports. Obviously this guy didn't shit where he ate. Come to think of it, he must eat in Greenland. Still, this exercise in visual imagery was getting me nowhere. I'd made my bed so I decided to settle back. I rested my head on his shoulder while his free hand went south again. He slid down my zipper. I was too smashed to do anything but let him.

I thought of Greg. What if they cancelled his gig due to bad weather? What if he came home early? What if he called our friends, the hospitals? He'd be worried no matter how much we'd drifted apart the past few months. My older self would have told this jerk to turn back, or pull over and "Let me out," but not the thirty-one-year old. No, I was already planning ahead, concocting a story even I wouldn't believe. Besides I'd never been to Madison.

I would tell Greg the next afternoon I'd stayed over at David's, too tired to make it home in the storm. And of course, being a close friend to us both, Greg would have already called David. He said he was fed up with my shit, all the jive. We argued and the rift between us grew wider, until there was nothing for me to do later, after several failed attempts to recapture what we'd once had, but pack my bags and head for the airport— back to California and the spare bedroom in my mother's new home with my ex-Marine-highway-patrol stepdad, and with zero prospects for work.

The snow on the windshield became thicker, wetter. The Manilow fan focused his eyes on the icy road ahead, his hands gripping the wheel at ten and two. I listened to the whoosh-whoosh of the wipers and the muted sounds of Diana Ross. "Do You Know Where You're Going To" was *my* song now. *Wasn't I proving it with the Manilow fan?* Greg couldn't stand the lyrics and refused to listen to Diana's "silly soul searching," but that didn't stop me from secretly humming the tune when I was doing the dishes or dreaming up potential lesson plans. Maybe Greg sensed I was already gone, that it would only be a matter of days before we'd finally split up. Funny how in retrospect everything seems to be about us. More likely it wasn't about me at all. Greg just didn't like the song.

THOMAS
JEFF MANN

(for Cynthia Burack)

WE SAID OUR goodbyes twenty years ago today. As poorly as I remember numbers, I remember that date: the 19th of September. The day of my greatest loss, really. Still, my memory is as unreliable as anyone else's, so, for the sake of accuracy, I've dug through dusty boxes of old journals for confirmation. Yes, my entry for September 20, 1991, reads:

Washington, D.C. 6:50 A.M.. He's gone. For all intents and purposes. Leaving Monday. I refused—unable to see him privately again—to hang around this weekend, to put on the ultimate acting job and see him with Dick. My sense of time is disjointed. Can it be only seventeen hours since he came into my office at two P.M. yesterday to tell me Dick got the job in Boston? That time between now and then seems not short, not long, just somehow nonexistent. Hours on the road, for the most part. Fleeing. When I return, he will be gone. Soon I will have lived with this for twenty-four hours. Somehow that amazes me, as the work traffic thickens along Connecticut Avenue, as the coffee dews my wild-length moustache, as dawn spreads across an almost cloudless and completely indifferent and unchanged sky over D.C.

"We said our goodbyes twenty years ago today." It's the sort of coincidence and symmetry we writers relish, and an attention-grabbing way to start this essay. Still, trying to read the scrawled notes my much younger self made so long ago, I'm stung, even after two decades, by that old pain: loving Thomas, conducting that hot, hot, furtive affair for six months behind his partner's back, then having to say goodbye.

▲

TODAY, THE 19ᵀᴴ of September 2011, is unremarkable. I took notes for this essay. I drove John, my partner of fourteen years, downtown to get his car serviced. After lunch, I started this essay. Later, I'll try to lift weights in our basement gym, if my aging back permits. Then, come five P.M., we'll get a good buzz on with a couple of martinis, followed by some leftover Chinese delivery and a Netflix DVD. This is a typical day for me: routine, unexciting, the placid life of a middle-aged writer/academic.

That 19th of September—the afternoon Thomas came to my Virginia Tech office to tell me his partner Dick had been offered a job in Framingham, Massachusetts, and they were already packing—that was another matter, one of those momentous days that change everything. Its significance seems so far removed from my present existence that it feels like some other man's history, some other man's sorrow. Still, much of what I've become is because of that day's leave-taking.

▲

THOMAS AND I were introduced by a mutual friend in Virginia Tech's War Memorial Gym in February 1991. He was twenty-seven, partnered, a graduate student in horticulture; I was thirty-one, single, an English instructor. We shared eccentric interests in neopaganism and the occult. I grew fond of both him and Dick, sharing relaxed evenings with them drinking, cooking, watching television. My attraction to him grew powerful, but I refused to act on it since he was coupled. Then one April evening, we attended a reading Allen Ginsberg gave at Radford University. Dick had campus connections, and afterwards we split several pitchers of beer at BT's, a student pub, with the famous author. When Thomas's leg brushed mine beneath the table, my leg rubbed his in return. Immediately my focus shifted from Ginsberg to less literary concerns.

The next day, Thomas and I confessed our reciprocal desire. Soon a secretive sexual relationship began. We made love roughly once a week, in a woodland cabin an acquaintance lent us. That summer, we even managed a get-away together, to Washington, D.C. and a conference of his at Penn State. Finally we were able to take our time, make love without watching the clock, and sleep all night side by side. In the mornings, I would wake before him, lift the sheet, and study his nakedness with silent reverence, thanking the gods that such a gift had been bestowed on me.

After years of almost constant celibacy, I was thoroughly besotted. I knew the pair was planning to leave Blacksburg once Thomas finished his master's degree in horticulture and they'd found jobs elsewhere. Rather than encouraging me to be cautious and retain some detachment, this knowledge only made me love him harder, more deeply, more desperately. Somehow I sensed that I'd never encounter such a passion again, and I was determined to live it to the hilt as long as I could, despite the guilt I felt in deceiving Dick, despite the looming loneliness bound to come. My desire for Thomas and our imminent parting inspired me to write poem after poem, all of them longing, erotic, and elegiac. There I was, in the grand tradition of the love poets I admired: Yeats, Keats, Shakespeare. It was a once-in-a-lifetime ardor and inspiration, I thought. I was right.

▲

THOMAS WAS MY erotic ideal, a short, muscular, scruffy-faced, hairy, butch bottom. To my gratitude and delight, he shared my predilection for kink, meaning that our sex usually involved rope and gags. Making love to him was perverse, delicious, and intoxicating. To see him naked, bound spread-eagle to the bed, gnawing the bandana knotted between his teeth, ready to submit to whatever I chose, was, for me, beauty beyond compare. To rest my face in the thick brown fur between his substantial pecs was as close to an earthly paradise as I've ever known. To give him up left me in the midst of a pain worse than any I've felt before or since.

To this day, despite the many, many men I've known carnally, despite my solid relationship with John, Thomas remains the great passion of my life. John—steady, orderly, meticulous—grounds, protects, and supports me. He makes for us a comfortable, beautiful home, a life where we can pursue our busy professional careers and profoundly relax once those overfull days are done. He is the perfect mate for my middle years. Thomas—fascinating, impish, mercurial—maddened, haunted, and stimulated me. He was the perfect muse for my youth. Though I may yet surprise myself by falling into a midlife affair equally as foolish as that long-ago relationship with Thomas, I think not. My fervid love for him seems to have burnt out in me the capacity to feel so deeply.

▲

MY JOURNAL PROVIDES me with details of that September parting I had forgotten. Reading my own words, I feel deep pity for the self I used to be, the hopeful boy with the beard much blacker than the one I wear today, the boy about to descend into that terrible sense of loss, bodilessness, and abandonment, about to pay the price for loving someone already spoken for.

Thomas is wearing jeans and a blue button-down shirt, over the top button of which curls brown chest hair. I lock the door behind him; we sit face to face. I'm quietly terrified, knowing that Dick has recently had a job interview in New England. Realizing how bereft I'm soon to be, Thomas tries to play down his excitement over moving to the Boston area, but soon enough he's chattering about the leather bars, the gargoyle store, the occult bookshop. No chance of another tryst or one last lovemaking, he explains. He and Dick will be too busy packing.

I break down, leaning against him, pressing my face against his chest, finally resting my head in his lap. With great effort, I choke back sobs. I'm the Top, the big butch mountain man; I should be strong and stoic in the face of this! My tears flow nevertheless. He holds me, without words, stroking my hair. His eyes are dry, but he swallows hard again and again. When I start fumbling for a Kleenex, he pulls one from his pocket, ever prepared. "Is this what you're looking for?"

Even in such extremity, I'm verbose. I want him to know what our too-brief connection has meant to me. I talk about the poetry he's inspired, how he's helped me escape the unlived life Henry James warns against in *The Ambassadors*. It's all been about touching beauty, I say, finally finding someone worthy, feeling more deeply than ever before, knowing this pain is just part of it. "With you, will all your gifts withdraw?" I quote from one of my own poems. No, no, some gifts will remain; I've got to believe that. He's the most exciting, intelligent, complex, desirable man I've ever known; I've learned so much…

Finally I say it, what he surely knows but what I've never verbalized. "I love you." To my stunned amazement, he replies, "I love you too." It seems unbelievable, finally to hear it, but to hear it mere minutes before we part.

We agree to keep in touch. He'll call collect sometimes, so that the call won't show up on a bill Dick might see. I wipe my eyes. One last hug before I unlock my office door. He looks up at me with what I take to be beaming fondness. I look down at him with a devotion I can only hope he doesn't perceive as pathetic. "With those boots on, you look ten feet tall!" he jokes. We shake hands on the steps of my office building. Seductively, cruelly, he tickles the inside of my palm with his middle finger. He strides across the Drill Field, and I watch him go. He looks back once, then disappears behind a line of trees. I stand in the sun, panting in the warm scent of junipers, trying to remember the smell of his armpits after vigorous lovemaking.

My eyes are red from crying, so I teach my next class wearing sunglasses. That evening, desperate for some kind of consolation, I drive to Washington, D.C., listening to Nanci Griffith's *Late Night Grande Hotel* again and again. When I cry, tear-spots spatter my glasses, like the salt stains left on winter pavement. The broken lines in the middle of the interstate say *subtraction subtraction subtraction*. I spend a few days with my best friend Cindy. She's given me advice during the last six months of my up-and-down feelings, my stint as The Other Man, loving someone I can cherish only for hurried assignations. She understands.

⚝

I WANTED NO one else for a long time. No one else measured up. Men who resembled him—who possessed his compact form, high brow, or wavy brown hair—only honed my grief. We kept in touch as promised, via letters and the rare phone call. He sent me gifts that helped me cling to the hope that he might one day leave Dick and come to me: an onyx pentagram ring, a Valentine's Day bear with devil horns. (Appropriate, since I'd always called him my demon lover, my Mephistopheles, making me, of course, a Faustus willingly bargaining his soul.) Upon the bear was imprinted the words I was so frantic to hear and to see: "I Love You."

Truth be told, September 19, 1991 was the day of our first goodbye. There were actually two other partings, an admission that dilutes the epic importance of the first. In March 1992, I drove to Framingham to visit Thomas and Dick. I had become a consummate actor and liar by then; ethics and honor meant nothing in the face of the passion I felt. While Dick was at work, Thomas and I enjoyed more ardent lovemaking. We shared a matchless erotic chemistry that, to this day, sad to say, I've found with no one else. Being with him again was sheer rapture, but in the end it only reminded me of all I was missing and how much more I wanted. I was in too much pain to continue the contact, I told him. The next day, I left the couple to their life together and drove back to Virginia and a bitter celibacy.

In the aftermath, I listened to Melissa Etheridge's lovelorn early CD's and sad country music like Vince Gill's "Never Knew Lonely." I took walks in the rain. I drove mountain back roads, wishing I had the strength to drive into a hillside. I was, obviously, a romantic cliché. Thomas's absence was all devouring. To have had such a passionate, beautiful lover and then not to have him, not to have anyone? For some deity to have allowed my body to awaken to such pleasure only to rob me of it seemed to me cosmic sadism without excuse. (At age fifty-two, I can barely comprehend my own past suffering, though, writing this, I can feel the slightest edge of it.) Family, friends, work, the simple pleasures of eating and drinking, none of them dulled that pain, though they were sufficient, just barely, to keep me from suicide, which I contemplated regularly, albeit lazily.

In 1995, Thomas wrote me, telling me that he and Dick had moved to Falls Church, Virginia. He missed me, he said; he wanted to see me. I fell back into it. We shared two weekends in February and May while Dick was out of town. I remember more amazing lovemaking, working Thomas' nipples with clamps, fucking him on his back, his thighs locked about my waist. I remember a stroll on Roosevelt Island, an evening concert at the Kennedy Center, the silver beginning in his beard. I remember fights, caused, I suspect, by my desperate desire to feel closer to him, feel indispensable, achieve a truer intimacy, and his profound need to keep some distance, guard himself, not get in too deep.

Finally, I remember one last lovemaking in Cindy's Cleveland Park apartment, a sweaty July afternoon after I'd returned from a sojourn in the British Isles. Thomas and I drank mead from quaichs I'd brought from Scotland. I licked Atholl Brose liqueur from his chest hair and the tip of his cock.

"You're a wonderful lover," he panted in our semen-sticky aftermath. As young, obsessive, and fervent as I was, I suspect he was right. I desired him more than any man before or since, and that focus must have translated into inventive and enthusiastic ways to give him pleasure.

After that, things fell irredeemably apart. The autumn of 1995, we quarreled over petty things via the new medium of e-mail. Then he and Dick broke up, and Thomas did what I could never forgive: After all I'd suffered loving him, he took a new boyfriend rather than come to me. Eventually, he and Dick got back together. By then I'd decided, after nearly five years of such agonizing ardor, that I'd finally, finally, finally had enough. His last e-mail message was flirtatious, telling me about his new black leather jacket, how good it looked with his full beard and chest hair.

Many of the poems inspired by my love for him I published, in literary journals, then in chapbooks—*Bliss* and *Flint Shards from Sussex*—and in full-length collections—*Bones Washed with Wine*, *On the Tongue*, and my multi-genre book, *Loving Mountains, Loving Men*. There are even a few in my most recent collection, *Ash: Poems from Norse Mythology*. When I read those poems in public, I often joke about how artistically productive sleeping with someone else's spouse can be, though the emotional repercussions make the poems hardly worth it. I am not likely to write so many lyrics about any one man again. My love poetry is inspired by conflict and the crazing inability to possess beauty and the beloved, and so my immoderate passion for Thomas created the ideal confluence of inspirational elements: yearning, remorse, sorrow. I don't expect to encounter such a "perfect storm" again. I say this with both regret and relief.

I got more than tortured poetry and a bevy of publications from Thomas. I learned a great deal: that my heart is attracted to complex, emotionally distant men, men who might inspire in me grand passion but who are, in the long run, not good for me; that I contributed as much to my own sad fate as Thomas did; that many people will take from you as much as you are willing to give; that suffering in the aftermath of a lost love maims you, perhaps irreparably, but opens your heart to others' suffering, thus making you more compassionate and more deeply human. That love and that loss were among the grand experiences of my life. I would do it all again, if only for the poems and the emotional growth.

▲

I HAVE SEEN him once since that final farewell. In January 2007, my publishers arranged a dual reading for famed author Patrick Califia and me in a San Francisco bookstore. There were two men already sitting in the foldout chairs when I arrived. One, a short, gray-bearded guy, gave me a huge smile. It wasn't until I was in the restroom that I realized who it was. Much of the old feeling came back. Had I been younger, less solid in my sense of self, I would have panicked. As it was, I wanted to stay in the bathroom and cry. Instead, I came out, acted as if everything were fine, and then very deliberately read material, both prose and poetry, based on my affair with Thomas. I did a fine job, if I may say so myself. The event I had dreaded for years had come to pass—crossing paths with him again—yet I was composed.

After I read, I joined the audience while Patrick took his turn. Anyone watching me would have assumed I was listening. Certainly my partner John, sitting only a few feet from me, had no idea how stunned I was. But actually I was studying Thomas. He was no longer the beautiful young man I had loved so wildly, for whom I had suffered such sorrow. He was no longer in his late twenties. He was in his mid-forties. He was plump, even grayer than I. I felt pity for him, and pity for myself, and pity for all mortal, aging beings. That was the last gift that loving him gave me, that sweeping, oceanic compassion. Thomas, the man with whom I had hoped to share my life, sat beside

John, the man with whom I've shared my life. I studied them both, heart swelling, and knew how soon our generation would lay down its turn at passion and shuffle off into the shadows.

After the reading, he approached me. "I'm Thomas!" he blurted.

"Oh, I know who you are," I said, mustering the defense of a sardonic tone. He introduced me to his new partner, who ironically turned out to be a fan of my writing, and then to Dick and his new partner. Thomas and Dick had broken up at last, long after it would have done me any good. After all the deceit, Dick still came to my reading. Obviously he had a much greater capacity for forgiveness than I ever would. And he had the last laugh, in a manner of speaking. He hadn't aged at all.

I fled after that. Southerners are pretty good at summoning false facades, and the affair with Thomas had honed my natural talent for duplicity, but my calm composure was splintering fast. "That was Thomas," I said to John as he and I headed across Market Street with Patrick and his adorable boy for a few drinks.

"*That* Thomas?" John gasped.

I drank a lot of Tullamore Dew that night. When John and I returned to our romantic guesthouse, I watched the gas fire flicker and couldn't sleep. Back home, I got an e-mail from Thomas, saying, among other chatty things, "I hoped you would have gotten over it long ago and would have been up for a beer and catching up."

I fell into a depression of several months' duration. My sex drive left me. I had no desire to be touched. Seeing Thomas had robbed me of my last illusion: That he, were we ever to meet again, would admit what a mistake it had been to leave me, how much he'd loved me, how much I haunted him. No. The relationship that had meant so much to me I'd always feared had meant very little to him, and now I knew that to be true.

⋏

SEPTEMBER 19TH WAS not the first Thomas-anniversary of 2011. The first was February 5th, twenty years since the day we met. This date I could not remember and had to look up in my journals. I spent that Saturday with pleasant distractions, visiting my old friend, Cindy, and her wife, Laree, in D.C. To Cindy, I explained the significance of the day. John I spared. In the first months of our relationship, he'd heard so much about Thomas that he'd politely but firmly asked me to stop talking about him. Seemed fair. I've honored that, except for rare and passing references to "The Demon Seed," "The Mythical Thomas," or "He Whose Name Must Not Be Mentioned." The letters, the empty bottles of mead and Atholl Brose, the devil-bear and pentagram ring, a pair of worn underwear, and a photo album, I keep discreetly packed away.

A couple of weeks after that twenty-year mark, I had lunch with a friend, Donnie, at the Radford bar BT's. It was the first time I'd been there since the night Thomas and I played footsie beneath the table after the Ginsberg reading. When Donnie arrived, I was reminded of how much he resembles a young Thomas. In fact, Donnie's about the age Thomas was when we met in 1991. He's short, butch, black-bearded, muscular, and very, very hairy.

I'm intimately acquainted with his lush body hair because sometimes, when John's out of town, Donnie shares my bed. Turns out I'm no more capable of monogamy than Thomas was, a fact John grudgingly tolerates. After I top Donnie, I lie there, that furry, handsome, burly boy in my arms, and watch him sleep. It's almost as if the miserly universe, after making me wait for two decades, has finally decided to honor the fidelity of my feelings by giving me some version of Thomas back.

At BT's, Donnie and I split a plate of chicken wings. He had worries; I gave him advice. He's a son of sorts, one of my boys, someone I want to take care of and protect. I'm not in love with him, though I love him. The desperate need and half-addled longing I felt for Thomas aren't there, just warm fondness, and gratitude, that an old Daddybear like me has such a buddy, a young man who's willing to share his beautiful body.

In the parking lot we hugged before Donnie headed back to classes. I drove home, listening to my favorite country-music star Tim McGraw singing "Everywhere." Something about that convergence—a young version of Thomas at BT's—had allowed for resolution. A tension in my heart eased up and laid down its bitterness, as if deciding that twenty years of mourning were finally enough. What I was left with, on that sunny February day, after all my fervid passions and attachments, my long history of deep loving, was a welling sense of thanks.

Ballad Echoes
Erik Orrantia

JORGE HAD A deep gash on either wrist, with thick black stitches at every quarter inch holding the pieces together crudely like leather flaps. The wounds were indicative not of some tentative cry for help but of utter determination to end it all. The viral blood that spewed from his arms in pulses that night stained the grout on the tile floor and also my memory.

▲

I MET JORGE on a busy Saturday night in El Butterfly, a happening club just outside of the Salto de Agua metro station in downtown Mexico City. I pushed through the crowd of mostly jeans and T-shirt-wearing twenty-somethings with my friend Gina ahead of me. He was standing there in a black sport coat and a button-up shirt. He looked over at me, stopping his conversation as I walked by. (I'll never forget his brown eyes, Aztec nose, and dark complexion, or the way his gaze followed me as I passed.) The music was still blaring—I hadn't heard it until I snapped back into the present, the throng of bodies around me twisting to the rhythm, and Gina a few impossible steps in front of me. When I finally caught up to her, we were far removed from him. I escorted her back to the table before I said determinedly, "I gotta go back."

I had been at the university in Mexico City for only a month or so, and had already dated a few serious letdowns. The population seemed to be divided into rich, egotistical swindlers and honest, humble, poor folk. Jorge was the best of both worlds, so I thought—chivalrous, funny, sincere, and employed full time at a bank. We agreed on meeting soon afterward at a place where sobriety and tranquility would allow us to get to know each other.

He doted on me the first night. He took me to the Mexican version of a country bar where he ordered up beer by the pitcher and we danced to twangy tunes. He wouldn't let me pay a single peso, and he taught me a couple of new line dances and the basic steps of cumbia. He had confidence in his hands when he danced, the kind of leader who let you know who was in charge. His shoulders felt firm and his posture strong on that first night of many back in 1997 in Mexico City, in *his* territory.

A week or so later, upon my request, he took me to a cemetery on the outskirts of the city. I was drawn by the mixture of serenity and sadness, growth and death, love and pain. I liked to read the epitaphs on the headstones of the young and old. Three or four words or maybe a sentence could sum up a person's existence: *Loved and admired. Died of spina bifida. Gone from us to God. I have HIV*. The latter wasn't on a gravestone. Jorge had chosen to tell me there among the graves, as good a place as any. He had just found out. His lips trembled as he uttered those words, and his eyes welled up with tears. The diagnosis explained the sudden, wordless disappearance of his ex. Jorge was afraid, of course, of the implications of the disease, and the possibility of losing me over it.

"You won't lose me because of HIV," I told him, as if I were taking on the challenge of dating a clashing astrological sign. I came from San Francisco, after all, where your chances of dating a positive guy were fifty-fifty. "You might lose me for other reasons, though."

Our relationship proceeded. He was truly a godsend.

Though his bank job turned out to be a sales position for shady retirement accounts, and he ended up leaving over his involvement in fraudulent exchanges, it gave him more time to show me around the world's largest metropolis. Not only did he become my personal tour guide of the city, but he also became my personal Spanish tutor. He dropped anything on the spur of the moment to accompany me, with or without my university group, to the far reaches of "D.F.," the Federal District. And he happily transcribed popular songs so that I might study them, starting with "Bésame," a song which desperately begged for a kiss, as if this were the last night of all.

The school year went by quickly. Before I knew it, May had rolled around. I had to return to San Diego, and Jorge and I had to make a decision. Simple enough. We had already lived together in D.F. for over six months. Tijuana offered serious benefits. Jorge would have access to better medical services with the help of San Diego charities, and I would be able to stay in Mexico to continue to improve my Spanish, integrate into the culture, stay with Jorge, and earn dollars in California. Perfect. We would move to Tijuana together.

I hadn't anticipated the concomitant shift in roles the move would create. For every place he had shown me in Mexico City, for every person he had introduced to me, for every ounce of energy he had exerted on me, and for every way I had depended on him, I now had to respond in triplicate. Before long, I became the provider of everything from the house, to food, transportation, acquaintances, and anything else he needed. But what I couldn't provide was impetus. Where was the confidence and strength I had seen in him? Where was the take-charge leader? I had removed a tropical bird from the jungle and expected it to fly and sing like it had in the trees. But Tijuana was a desert and this bird wouldn't fly. In the next two years, he hadn't changed a bit. He hadn't learned a word of English; he hadn't completed a single course of study; he hadn't found a stable job; and he hadn't learned to drive. My willingness to continue providing dwindled. I was getting bored.

Another song Jorge had transcribed for me began to permeate through my soul. "Yo No Sé Qué Me Pasó" means "I Don't Know What Happened." He once scolded me for singing it too emphatically, especially the part about not feeling love anymore. "You will suffer for a while, I know," the song continued, as did the compassionate tone of my voice. "Someone new will come along and give you his love." I was hurting inside, and the lyrics expressed what I was feeling.

It's not fair to say he hadn't changed at all. I started to see physical changes in him. He was receiving some medication from the local AIDS clinic (a different set of meds every month) and generally seemed healthy. But I noticed subtle changes, perhaps having nothing to do with the disease. He was putting on weight. He smelled different. His skin tasted bitter. He had fungus on his finger and toenails. He contracted anal warts from having cheated on me. Sex diminished between us. Then I cheated on him, too. I met Leon.

I started chatting with this guy online one day, a chance meeting of a man who said he worked at a travel agency. "Not looking for sex," he wrote, but he'd give me a great deal on an airline ticket. I was planning to go see my mother, so I took him up on it. I drove out to this little travel agency on the way to the airport and, sure enough, the guy gave me the ticket on the cheap. He was cordial to me but busy with other clients. Out of a door behind where he sat walked a lanky kid in a bathrobe, wearing crooked, black-framed glasses. Not very appealing. Cleaned up, he could be my type, though.

He sat across the counter from me, introduced himself as Leon, and started to make small talk. Even from there I could smell what my stepdad used to call dragon breath. He had gone out the previous night and suffered from a serious hangover. Still, he was bubbly, intelligent, and charming. In February 2001, Leon was twenty-one; I was thirty.

"I gotta go," I kept saying, mostly uninterested in him.

"Fine, leave me all alone," Leon responded. I stayed all afternoon. He was fun and magnetic.

Before long, I learned from Leon a new song called *"Eres Secreto de Amor"* or "You're a Secret of Love." Leon and I sang it as we grabbed each other's hands and legs beneath the tablecloth at a restaurant. Our respective boyfriends sat opposite us. I started visiting him at his downtown apartment early in the morning before work. He couldn't wait to strip off my clothes. I couldn't wait to absorb him with all my senses. It was wrong and stupid. I loved it.

The lines of Jorge's song echoed through my brain, telling me to be true to myself, to break up rather than continue on the way we were. I had fallen out of love with Jorge and had become undeniably embroiled with Leon. I couldn't be with Jorge anymore. I couldn't fake it. Yet I was committed to him. Period. I felt grateful to him, and I knew without me he had nothing. He had come to Tijuana for me. Though he had squandered his potential and we had let our relationship slip away, I couldn't bear to kick him out, nor did he choose to return to D.F. on his own.

Jorge's song said it was best to be the one to say goodbye first. The wisdom of the song, its poignancy, was crystal clear. Why didn't I listen? Why couldn't I have taken the responsibility as well as the guilt? I should have ended the relationship cleanly and let him suffer for a little while, knowing he would come out okay in the end. But I didn't.

Then Leon had to leave his apartment, so he moved in with me. Jorge migrated to the guestroom. I thought we could all get along, like friends. After all, I figured in my perfectly logical rationalizations, Jorge and I had grown apart anyway. The house was big enough, and Jorge had begun dating another guy. He'd get a job, become independent, and move on in his own time.

I miscalculated his feelings while I tried to cushion my own. And then the Scorpio came out in Leon. So much for taking on those clashing astrological signs. The other side of his magnetism and charm was manipulation. My daily routine consisted of leaving early in the morning to cross the border, working a stressful day with middle school children, and returning home to hear both sides of the story. *He said this. He did that. He pushed me. He tried to stab me with scissors. Erik, do something!* And I thought testicles were just for sex.

I had that trip to my mother's house. Spring vacation, if I recall correctly, and a chance for me to get away from it all. What's that saying? When the cat's away, the mice will play. Well, what do two angry cats do when the mouse runs off?

When I was in Michigan, Leon started calling me right away, waking up my parents in the wee hours of the night. It was embarrassing, the same trifles over which I would now have to preside from a long distance. *Jorge took clothes from the closet. Jorge locked the bathroom door.* I wished they would sort out a few things on their own. I wished they would leave me alone for a week. I wished Leon would stop waking up my parents or that my folks would shut off the phone.

My fifth night away, I received the fourth late night call. My older brother had already reprimanded me. "Don't you know it's rude for them to call at this time of night?" Of course I knew. I was mortified, perhaps as much by the impression this would give my family that my life was out of control as by my own realization that indeed it was. I wanted to break the phone or pull the wire from the jack.

"Phone for you," my mother said, entering the room, irritated again.

"Sorry," I whimpered. As soon as she shut the door, I was ready to explode. "Stop fucking calling me!" *Enough was enough!*

Leon's somber voice: "Jorge tried to kill himself."

I was stupefied. "What do you mean?" I managed as I sat up in bed. He explained the whole story: Leon had gone out with a friend to the bars downtown. They ran into Jorge there. The situation was awkward. The friend split, leaving Leon and Jorge alone together in the bar. Jorge had already had a number of drinks. But they were polite to each other and, strangely, seemed to be getting along well. They both kept drinking until Jorge, totally inebriated, could no longer function. He began to cry hysterically. Leon had little choice but to take him away from there so he loaded him in a taxi and took him home.

Half an hour later, they arrived at the house far removed from the bar but not far from the drunkenness. Jorge stumbled inside. Things were okay until he saw an empty wine bottle in the kitchen with a wilted rose in it. He mustn't have seen it there before. He must have guessed it was a gift from me to Leon or Leon to me. He didn't know it was a present from a female friend of Leon. He went berserk.

His crying became a tirade. He ranted around the house with the empty bottle in his hand. Upstairs, downstairs, back to the kitchen and then to the living room where Leon stood, as if in the middle of a stage during a live theater act. Crash! Jorge threw the bottle on the tile floor and the bottle exploded in a thousand green shards, the red rose in the center of the carnage.

Jorge, with a swaying head, surveyed the pieces and picked up the biggest chunk of glass he could find. The sharpness of the amorphous shard matched that of any razor; it sliced easily through both his wrists. Leon watched in horror as blood spurted in pulsing throbs, leaving a splattering of dark red circles all about the broken glass. Leon knew the blood was tainted, dangerous. But Jorge would die if he didn't do something. Leon stepped into the kitchen, crunching glass underfoot and smearing blood. He reached for a dishtowel.

"Wrap this around you!" he said frantically.

Jorge would not accept help; he ran from the kitchen and out the front door, leaving in his wake a crimson trail. Leon followed him outside, where he stopped on the sidewalk, watching as Jorge ran down the street and disappeared behind a corner.

Leon discovered later that some time after Jorge left, a Tijuana taxi driver spotted him sitting in the doorway of a business closed for the night. One can only imagine what he looked like there, hunkered over a pool of blood or lying in it, his wrists open like a mangled, sopping package. By some grace, the man got him into his taxi and drove him across town to the Red Cross.

"Fifteen minutes from dying," the doctor had said. He stitched up the wounds and gave him a pint or two of bagged blood. The cuts were deep like gashes in a tomato, with the seeds oozing out; I saw them when I got back from my mother's house. Jorge pulled back the gauze so I could see. He seemed neither reticent to show me nor embarrassed about it. *See what I did for you, or because of you?* I imagined him thinking, *See how I need you?* The cuts were jagged and grotesque, the thick black string stitched sloppily. This physical manifestation of the situation we had created made me queasy.

A few weeks later Jorge left. He found a small apartment and shacked up there with some guy. He took a menial job and they did what they could to make ends meet. I snuck away at times to see Jorge. I gave him money every month for a while to help out, and to make me feel better. His scars will never go away, and neither will mine. I still sigh when I think of the whole mess.

I broke up with Leon about three long years later. I'm a glutton for punishment. Those manipulative ways of his only got worse. And I let him lead me into one disaster after another. The fiasco with Jorge had been a foreshadowing of blunders to come; luckily, few of them involved blood.

Of course, I can't help but think of Leon and Jorge and the way they both made me a better person. Jorge had given me so much of his heart, perhaps the best part of it, though I wish he'd given that much heart to himself. I regret the idea that he's become a bitter person and likely blames me for the way our relationship turned out. I hear from his best friend in Mexico City that he's returned to the city and is okay after all this time. He won't talk to me. Just as well.

Leon taught me things I wish I didn't have to know. I use

my balls now when I need to. I defend myself. I don't endure as much crap from people as I used to. Now that he's disappeared, I'm afraid his dislikeable ways may have been an end to him. His final lesson to me, then, was balance. And I strive to balance those lessons within me—to stick up for myself without stepping on others. Some say that everything reverts to the Golden Rule.

▲

I AM WITH another lover, one of eight years now. I had doubted that I'd ever make it this far with someone. His name is Francisco and he loves music. I love whatever he listens to. Thankfully, he has learned English in our time together, drives a car, and runs an honest business—he's a very honest man. Our song is "Still the One" by Shania Twain. Yet I reminisce. Now and then I listen to those songs that defined those moments I have written about. Had I only known back then…had I only been strong enough to prevent those things from happening.

Am I strong enough now? I sit sometimes and wonder, while my lover is out for the night with his drinking buddies again. I reflect on an imperfect thing, a relationship, a job, a home, or a place. Life's filled with disappointment and pain. Then again, I don't appreciate what I have until I have lost it. Life is also filled with tough decisions because so little is black or white, so little is certain or perfectly clear. Yet after what I've been through, an unsettling sense tells me that I should have learned to tell when that situation, that relationship, that thing, is at least perfect enough, shouldn't I?

THE OTHER SIDE OF THE GAME
PHILIP DEAN WALKER

OUR AFFAIR BEGAN purely by chance. I'd seen Drew at the gym off and on for over two years. He was never really on my radar, just someone I knew of but only in a hazy, through-the-scrim kind of way, sort of like how you *know* of Brad Pitt's existence. I'd watched him in awe, always surreptitiously and by way of mirrors and covert glances from the water fountain, as he lifted huge barbells without even a simple grimace, the weight almost secondary to the graceful movements he made, a series of veins like ancient tributaries appearing in bas-relief from his shoulder to the end of his wonderfully massive forearms. Drew was the kind of perfectly sculpted god you could look at and admire from afar but were not allowed to touch—a living, breathing Roman statue walking amongst us, the mere peasantry.

His square, Germanic jaw and light green eyes gave him a mature, manly appearance that made him seem wise beyond his years (late twenties). He moved about the gym almost blissfully unaware that others were watching him, worshipping him, physically arrested during their own workouts by his unparalleled beauty. He was hot on a galactic scale. While everyone else, including myself, seemed to fumble about from machine to machine, Drew's workouts had an efficient, willowy choreography to them. I saw him in the gym, but I was quite sure he didn't see me.

Drew was a successful personal trainer, an ex-Marine with a boyfriend of almost two years who was in college, and he drove a silver Mercedes. These were all personal details I'd learned from one of my friends, Carl, who had been admiring Drew from afar for years.

"What I wouldn't do for one night with him, my God," he would say. "You know that you're totally his type, don't you?"

As I placed forty-five-pound weights on either side of the bar for a warm-up set, then straddled the bench to practice my form, I caught a glimpse of myself in one of the many mirrors the attentive staff at Results Gym on U Street had installed around the gym. I was proud of the physical transformation I'd accomplished, and if the looks from other guys in the locker room were any true gauge, people were noticing. In four years, I'd successfully managed to put on over forty pounds of mostly lean muscle, replacing an almost emaciated frame with ripples of muscle, a six-pack, and a pair of broad, meaty shoulders. Still rather lean and tall, I carried the new look well and had felt my sexual currency rise within the tightly woven gay neighborhood of Dupont Circle. I was particularly proud of my biceps, which were now large and well proportioned where at one time I'd pathetically been able to encircle my thumb and index finger around them.

Drew was lifting barbells in front of a set of mirrors that ran perpendicular to my bench. His white tank top hugged his V-shaped frame without appearing skin-tight. I noticed it was the same top he often wore to workouts. I was wearing a dark blue Nike cross-country singlet with mesh holes on the sides acting as air vents as well as a pair of tight white soccer shorts that accentuated my glutes. A gay gym is like a singles bar, but with weights instead of cocktails: You have to look your most fuckable at all times.

I banged out twelve reps for my first set and turned the volume up on my iPod a couple notches to syncopate my exercise with the smooth, wailing sounds of "Other Side of the

Game," a live Erykah Badu song. I loved the slow build-up of the song, how Badu takes her time with it, goading the audience with the first coy stanzas, which then lead to a crescendo of voices, hers rising to the top like a siren, commanding the lyrics and pulsing the emotion through my ear buds as I lifted. It was an eight-minute song that I often put on repeat, convinced it somehow made me lift more weight. It was a placebo tune, one that inspired confidence and bravado that I tried to use to my advantage in the testosterone charged gym, imbued with the rapid pulse of male sexuality and endless cruising. Every workout seemed like it could potentially end in sex. And it often did.

As I racked the weight onto the bar for a third set, I realized that I'd definitely need a spot. I'd made the mistake in the past of being too confident, foregoing a spotter and then failing in the middle of a rep, mortified as I rolled out from underneath a weighted bar that threatened to crush my sternum while other lifters watched agog.

Drew walked back from the water fountain to his own lifting station and passed right in front of me just as I had been looking around for a staff member to help me through my final set. What happened next would monumentally change the rest of my life.

"Excuse me. Would you mind spotting me?" I asked as he walked in front of my bench.

"Of course." He smiled such a wide, welcoming smile that it seemed to instantly change his entire persona—from unapproachable and god-like to warm and friendly. Up close, I noticed that his lips were imminently kissable. "How many reps?" he asked as he got behind me and the bench, his crotch now only inches away from my face.

"I'm going for eight."

"Okay, so ten then." He smiled again and I was high on the fumes of what I was starting to believe might have been a mutual flirtation. My whole body felt electric and turned on, the nerve endings tingling.

I pushed through the first seven reps with no problem at all, coasting on a mixture of confidence, nervousness, and adrenaline. Then I started to struggle. Drew placed his fingers underneath the bar. Without actually helping me, the effect of his guiding the bar up and down, got me through the rest of my set of twelve reps—a new personal best with that weight.

Sliding off the bench, I thanked him.

"I'm Drew," he said, taking off his lifting glove and putting his hand out for a handshake. "It's great to meet you." That wide smile again and his affable disposition were so complementary to the perfection of his physique, it was quite possible, I thought at that moment, that I had just met the perfect man.

"I'm Phil. Thanks a lot for the spot."

"See you around," Drew said and walked away. And with that, something akin to a seismic shift in the Earth's plate tectonics propelled me through the rest of my workout.

▲

WHEN I CAME home from the gym, I looked up Drew on Friendster. It was 2007 and Facebook had not yet taken its position as the premiere social networking site of the universe. I reviewed some of the basic information under his profile: *27 years old. Personal Trainer. Hometown: Upstate New York.* In a Relationship. I took note of the relationship status and then quickly moved on from it.

Beyond Friendster, Drew was a surprisingly easy person to find online. There were endless pictures of him in varying degrees of undress, including what looked like a fashion spread in a magazine, the January issue of a popular gay monthly. He was on the cover in a David Bowie T-shirt with the sleeves cut off, his biceps bulging and wearing white pants and a black belt. His clearly prominent package was covered by big, bold red letters: *White Hot! Cover Guy Drew Inverness Warms Us Up This Winter.* He had a come-hither look, yet his eyes still had that kindness I had seen in them at the gym that day we first met. The rest of the photos featured him shirtless and up against a wall, as well as a profile shot in which he wore a leather vest opened up to accentuate his abdominal muscles. In the last picture, Drew was photographed sitting against a yellow-painted cinderblock wall, legs splayed amidst what looked like white garden rocks. A large, spindly plant seemed to crane one of its tendrils toward his Calvin Klein boxer-briefs. My lord, who was this guy?

I Googled him. One of the first sites listed was an eBay auction. People were actually bidding on the magazine. On another site, he was the topic of a discussion thread on male models. It was unreal; this hot guy seemed to have his own fan base. What chance could I possibly have?

But I felt we'd made a connection at the gym, and I knew I had to follow-up on it regardless of the outcome. An electrically charged pulse had been exchanged between us when we shook hands and locked eyes—that moment you hear about when someone describes meeting their soul-mate or see in a movie when Harry meets Sally or Rhett takes notice of the self-consciously coy Scarlett. I seemed to have only cinematic points of reference for what I thought had occurred. But had it even really happened? Was I just another doting admirer to whom Drew had thrown a quick boyish grin as a sort of consolation prize? He must've known the effect he had on those around him. How could he not?

I sent him a brief, but specific, Friendster message: "It was great to meet you. Thanks for the spot."

His response the next day was a shocker: "Anytime! I've seen you there before and have been wanting to spot you for quite some time! LOL. Anyway, stop looking so cute...it distracts me from my workouts. Drew."

The needle went off the record for me at that point. I stopped hearing things around me and could only stare into a wide, fantastic void of possibility that had suddenly opened up, a multi-colored slide into a porn-laden fantasy world where every touch ended in ecstasy and I was finally with the hottest guy in school. Wait. Let me get this straight, I said to myself. You have been on *his* radar the whole time? The very idea was preposterous, insane, somehow out of the physical realm of possibility. I had to keep this conversation going, but I wasn't sure how to reply.

Finally, I suggested we work out the next weekend. He wrote back saying that workouts were his alone time; without fail, he'd end up training his lifting partner and neglect his own workout. He suggested instead that we meet for a post-workout dinner. I couldn't have replied faster. The next Saturday we'd both work out and then head out for dinner. It was a date. An actual date. Dinner. And *he* had asked *me*. I was on top of the world. And I was terrified.

▲

IN THE WEEK leading up to our date, I was alternately excited and cautious. There was now a certain deliciousness to the ordinary that hadn't been there the week before. Still, I had questions. I took off the rose-colored goggles for a moment and started looking at the facts: A guy with a boyfriend had asked me out. Okay, so what exactly did that mean? What did that make me? I decided not to worry as the boyfriend was not my problem. Logistically speaking, I was his.

To distract myself, I went shopping. I bought a brand-new outfit to wear to the gym for that coming Saturday, a blue tank top with red piping that showed off my pecs and a nice, snug pair of shorts designed to accentuate my new bubble butt— when you gain forty pounds of muscle, everything is "new." I told my friend Carl about what had happened between Drew and me. He was jealous, but happy for me.

"I wouldn't have even taken a chance if you hadn't told me that I was his type," I said.

"Oh, great," he replied.

When I walked into the gym that Saturday, I headed straight for the incline bench intent on doing the exact same workout I'd been doing the last time we met. I can be superstitious like that. I was nervous. What was I going to say? I didn't have as much experience dating as I had hooking up. It was easier to just hop into bed without a second thought than to actually sit down and get to know someone.

I looked around at the usual array of mid-afternoon weekend, hardcore gym bunnies, saggy granddaddies lurking in the shadows, and the cute Alpha Gays sweating out their Rose Kennedys from the night before. At the time, Results on U Street took up three floors of an old warehouse and retained much of its 360-degree extended view on each level. Weights were arranged in an open plan, so a lifter could see anyone at any time, which is what made it such an infamous cruising spot in D.C.

Drew walked onto the gym floor at 3:30. He'd told me that he had clients until two o'clock in Virginia and then he'd make his way over. He was wearing a gray tank top with black basketball shorts and Saucony shoes. He looked downright edible.

"Hey, you," he said, his big, beautiful grin lighting up the entire room. "I was thinking I'd pick you up around six for an early dinner. I know this great Mexican place in Pentagon City."

I said that sounded perfect. Drew spotted me several times throughout my workout and looked over at me with an anticipatory look of delight in his eyes. I went through the rest of the workout in a kind of beautiful fog.

He picked me up in front of my apartment building at six on the dot. I was wearing a pair of jeans and what I liked to call my Spiderman shirt, a long-sleeved gray sweatshirt with blue webbing that made me look like the superhero. It fit tightly, as did most of my wardrobe. Drew wore a pair of khaki cargo shorts and a green Lacoste that hugged him tightly around his massive torso. The sleeves looked painted on his biceps. "Let's go," he said when I slid into the passenger seat. He had opened the door for me.

During dinner, Drew was very candid about his background. He had no relationship with his father, had only met him once, in fact. He and his brothers and a sister had grown up in subsidized housing in a small town in upstate New York with very little money. His mother was a waitress at a diner, and Drew had to fight the pressure to deal drugs in order to help support his family.

"I heard my mother crying one night after we'd all gone to bed. Right then and there I had made this pact with myself that I was going to buy her a house one day," he said.

Drew had an identical twin brother who was straight and still living where they grew up with a couple of children born out of wedlock. "Everything I do, all the success I've had, and I've had a lot, it's all for my family," he said. After the Marine Corps, Drew started work as a personal trainer and then quickly became one of the most sought after ones in the Washington D.C. area. He was also taking classes to get his college degree part-time.

He asked me about my background and I answered his questions with some trepidation. I downplayed certain aspects of my own story. My family has never suffered financially in my entire lifetime. I have never wanted for anything. I grew up in Great Falls, one of the most affluent suburbs of Northern Virginia in a house decorated like a museum by a mother who was an interior designer with exquisite taste. I went to high school with the children of diplomats, Senators, Supreme Court Justices. The student parking lot looked like a luxury vehicle dealership. I occasionally drove my dad's Mercedes to school. I attended Middlebury College, my first-choice school, and my grandmother paid for my entire education. She also bought me a car. She gave me my own credit card that I'd take to Georgetown with one of my friends and spend thousands of dollars recklessly on clothes we didn't need. It was a feckless, easy existence and the only hardship I could really recall, was a subterranean, toxic homophobia that existed within the tony bedroom community.

People who grow up financially secure tend to romanticize

poverty, especially the extreme kind of poverty it sounded like Drew came from. And if this were possible, Drew's meager origins made him even more attractive to me. Somehow, this entrepreneurial spirit he'd adopted to lift himself out of squalor and into his huge Logan Circle condo, the silver Mercedes, the impossibly hot body (because, of course, as I learned later, he'd been formerly fat as well), everything contributed to the mythical quality I'd built up around him.

One area we both seemed to consciously leave unexplored was the subject of his boyfriend. If I didn't bring him up, it was like he didn't really exist. Couldn't I just make him irrelevant? Couldn't I just replace him entirely?

After dinner, we went back to his place. He had two parrots that greeted us at the door. Drew let one of them perch on his finger and he kissed it while stroking its feathery neck. He had made his own recording studio and was an accomplished "mixer." Several of his remixes had even charted. As I was looking through his collection in his bedroom, he came from behind and put a hand on my ass. He turned me around and kissed me deeply, with those wide, plump lips that I'd noticed the first time up close. We then made love. And that was a first time for me— not the first time I'd had sex with a guy, but the first time I felt like I was "making love" and not getting fucked hard from behind from a guy who I didn't really care about. He held me in his arms all night. And in the morning, he drove me out to Great Falls, so I could have Easter brunch with my family.

The next two months were the happiest of my life. It's good to be able to pinpoint the time in which you were happiest. It's a question you're inevitably going to be asked and when most people have to think about it, you'll know exactly when your time was. You can take that memory out from time to time and look at it, and re-live it, re-experience it. The feeling never goes away, no matter how much time passes.

I was Drew's lover during that time in the spring of 2007 when his boyfriend was studying abroad in Europe. I played the role of the other man and it fit me like the proverbial glove. The other man can pretend he has his man's heart and can even fool himself that he'll leave his partner one day. But does the other man really have this kind of power? I'd seen "the other woman" ascend before, even in my own family. Couldn't I do the same?

We spent every weekend together, exploring every inch of our bodies. The way he made love to me was unlike any of my other partners. He was so careful, gentle, so loving. It was erotic and romantic. "You look like Prince William, you know that? You're like my prince," he said to me.

I tried to remember the exact choreography of our sessions together to recall later in my mind. After leaving his place on Saturday mornings, I'd often go to the Luna Grille on Connecticut Avenue and sit at the bar, order a big breakfast and listen to my iPod, conjuring up the events from the night before. I'd try to find my way inside that moment again, when Drew was in the deepest part of me and both of us were swept away, transported. We rarely, if ever, used condoms. That kind of risky behavior was not in my character, but he had a way of making me forget to take precautions.

Drew introduced me to his friends. He made me his "plus one" at events. He took me up to the rafters of a club where his friend was DJ-ing and made out with me, while a shimmering disco ball danced across our faces while we kissed. We'd go out to Dupont Circle on Sunday afternoons and nap together on the grass like a couple, do a little shopping, eat a light dinner at a new bistro on 17th Street and then return to his place. He'd wrap me up in his arms and not let go until the next morning.

He introduced me to his mortgage lender and his real estate agent.

"It's time to get you out of your studio apartment. The walls are closing in on you," he said.

"You're right. It's like an Indiana Jones movie," I replied, referring to the scene in *Indiana Jones and the Raiders of the Lost*

Ark when Harrison Ford is stuck in a cave and the walls are threatening to squish him into a pancake. We went house hunting like newlyweds. Drew was pushing me to move into a condo building being constructed not two doors down from where he lived.

One night, after visiting one of his friends, we sat in Drew's car and talked. Without much forethought, I brought up the one topic we had never broached.

"What's going to happen when your boyfriend comes back?" Once asked, I couldn't take the question back.

"Well, I guess we'll just pick up where we left off."

How matter-of-fact. "I am going to be devastated when that happens. You know that, don't you?"

"Phil, let's not think about it. Who knows what will happen? Remember I was the one who was after you all those months. Don't forget that."

When we made love that night, I didn't think about tomorrow.

▲

DREW LOVED THE navy blue mesh Nike singlet I'd been wearing the day we first met, so for his birthday I wanted to get him one. I called around and discovered that particular item had been discontinued. So, I hopped onto eBay and found a shirt just like mine—it was exactly his size. After the gift arrived, I went down to Georgetown and had it wrapped at The Paper Store on M Street in parrot wrapping paper and light blue ribbon.

That birthday night was to be our last one together. Drew's boyfriend was flying in the next morning. I tried to picture what it would be like the next time I saw Drew in the gym or, God forbid, ran into him in a club with that little blond twink boyfriend of his, but I couldn't. I put on a pair of jeans and a collared shirt with a little bumblebee logo on the right-hand side. Drew picked me up and we went out to dinner at Champs in Pentagon City. He had an unsophisticated palette and suggested mostly chain-type restaurants. He also could eat an entire pie or cake in one sitting if he wanted to.

When we returned to the car, I pulled the present from under the seat. He smiled at me and told me he couldn't believe I had remembered his birthday. He unwrapped the present. "I can't take your favorite workout singlet, Phil."

"It's not mine, Drew. I found one for you in your size."

He looked at me as if he were seeing *us* for the first time, or maybe just the possibility of us. I started to cry. I told him I didn't know how I was going to live after he went back to his boyfriend. I can't remember how many times we went back and forth about the whole thing, but I know that by the end of it I was a sobbing mess. Drew took me back to his place and we made love one last time and in the morning he took me home. The next day at the gym, I got a text message from him saying he was wearing the singlet and thinking of me. I tried to hold on to that.

The rest of that weekend was a dark, devastating blur of nihilism and end-of-the-world thoughts filled with self-indulgent music and crying—histrionic sobbing complete with me curled up into a fetal position on the floor, wrapped in my comforter. Brooke Logan had just been raped on *The Bold and the Beautiful*—Stephanie Forrester, Brooke's arch-nemesis, had unwittingly arranged it. As I watched the TV show, I sobbed for her anguish. Her pain was my pain. It was ridiculous of me. I was unfamiliar with the emotional jet lag one experiences in going from such a high to such an unfathomable low in a short amount of time. I had tasted this heavenly fruit and then was banned from the one store selling it.

Two months later in August, Drew called me on a Sunday while I was reading *Looking for Mr. Goodbar*. He sounded frantic and somewhat unhinged. "Guess what happened?"

I have to admit that I immediately knew what he was going to say next. "He dumped me," he said. I had to fight to keep the joy out of my voice. "I'm driving back right now from New

York. Can I come over tonight?"

He showed up at my door pale and red-eyed. He'd clearly been crying all day. He collapsed into my bed and I held him. His solid body felt fragile and acquiescent to my touch. For the first time, he seemed broken, not strong. He cancelled his morning clients and convinced me to call in sick to work so I could spend the day in bed with him. There he was, finally unattached and lying down next to me, and with no one else to care for him. But how long would even this moment last?

And where do I go from here? Do I recount how the condo I had bought pre-construction next to Drew's building had a fire and that I had to walk away from my entire investment? Do I explain that I was so in love with him that I let him convince me to go out to a club one night and spy on his boyfriend for him because he thought his boyfriend was seeing someone new? Do I mention that I took pictures of them that night and sent them to Drew and that Drew showed up at the club to see for himself? And that I used his grief that night to seduce him again? Do I go on to explain that I slept with him for four more years, off and on, after that? That I'd drop men who cared about me, guys I was seriously dating and genuinely liked, just so I could sleep with him again? Can I say that I still wish him happy birthday every year through text messages and hope every year that he'll do the same for me? Do I dare tell you what happens to the other man who won't let go?

THREE'S A CHARM
WES HARTLEY

MY BOYFRIEND RILEY and I met the first time on a halibut fishing trip when he had just turned sixteen. This was two summers ago when Riley's Uncle Ronny and I were still an item. Riley had wheedled his uncle into including him in our annual saltwater safari. Nephew said he'd always wanted to tangle one-on-one with a trophy muscle-fish. Uncle Ron felt pretty sure that sporty Nephew could handle the marathon action so we brought him along.

Riley tied into a 160-pound halibut. It fought him for almost two hours, but Riley hung in there and won the contest. We had to use the wench on the charter boat to heft the monster flatfish on board. The muscular halibut weighed as much as muscular Riley. Riley earned his rite-of-passage bragging rights and got a firsthand insider peek into sport fishing male-bonding and boyfriendly masculine camaraderie.

I had definite inklings about Riley's likely orientation during that introductory outing, but I didn't mention it to Ronny. Ron was righteously standing in as a surrogate masculine daddy-substitute for Riley. Ron's absentee older brother had knocked up Sister-In-Law and took off to the States before Riley was even born. Ron had been there for Riley since the beginning. I didn't think it was a good idea at the time to clue-in over-protective Uncle on my take on Nephew's gaydar signaling and roving baby blue eyes, which turned out to have been a good plan.

Over the next two years, every time Ron would include Riley in the mix, or whenever Riley and I would cross paths in the neighborhood, I'd be on the receiving end of his teenage hormonal broadcasting, but I'd always try to deflect it however I could—which wasn't easy since Riley was super aggressive and persistent just like his avuncular guardian. All these undercover fireworks were a lot to juggle for a wobbly third wheel like Yours Truly, but somehow I managed.

I didn't know a lot about Riley's home life or upbringing except what Ronny had told me about his sort-of-sister-in-law being a single parent and certain details about his own ongoing role as conscientious masculine surrogate. Riley knew his uncle had a serious boyfriend but that was about the extent of it. Ron had his own apartment and employment scenario and routine, and I had mine. We were definitely hooked up, but not ready to move in together and set up housekeeping. This arrangement worked for both of us pretty well for two years and it also made our unplugging rather more amenable than it might have turned out under different circumstances. Riley had taken all this in and rolled with it in his own way.

Long-story-short, pretty quick after Ron and I got past our mutually amicable split-up—just after Riley's high school grad actually—Riley showed up at my door one Saturday night looking for some adult masculine input on a certain important topic, more than a little curious, and apparently looking to replace Uncle Ronny in my boyfriendly preoccupation. Or, that's what I was thinking in the beginning.

Since Riley was still in his rookie closet, and since he was youngish and kind of related and had crowded in so soon after Ron and I broke up, this surprise move of his was very touchy and loaded with lots of potential issues. At first I couldn't figure how to proceed or whether I should spin my wheels or what I ought to do. Nothing was getting communicated in actual words—perspicuity is not Riley's strong suit—but through innuendo, indirection, and trial-and-error I finally got my bearings.

Come to find out Riley was looking for safe friendly trustworthy mentoring—congenial sexual uncle-nephew-style boyfriending without the baggage. He was leaving it up to me to show him the ropes and take care of the details. Riley liked me a lot and he knew I liked him a lot, too. He was trusting me to do right by him and be responsible sexually. Big order.

I suggested we keep his little secret between ourselves, while Riley insisted that our budding whatever-connection be kept totally confidential until he was ready to come out. He also let me know that he expected to call the shots. All this made a lot of sense to me in the beginning, so of course, I went along with it and decided to play it by ear. Under different circumstances the age difference could have been a controversial issue—more than fifteen years—but familiarity and chemistry trumped everything else and smoothed over any rough edges.

Riley is all boy. He's a hyper-masculine team sport jock-type. He's got lots of different sporty buddies. Riley and his buds are always "going for it" one way or another then afterwards hitting the showers. Wheels, boards, and balls, Riley says. And other stuff too I'm guessing. Riley sees himself as a winner. He's got an attitude. He appears to be Mister Popularity with his pals. It's easy to see Riley likes guys. He's all about guy-stuff and guys. Same as his Uncle Ronny.

Riley requires a lot of personal attention. He insists on being center stage at all times. He loves to get naked and strut his stuff for his appreciative admirer. The boy is under a lot of hormonal pressure and needs a lot of head. He obviously appreciates gifts and compliments but isn't into reciprocating anything. End of discussion. Riley's way into himself. Mister Perfect sees himself as a top. In Riley's definition that means getting regular head, but at this stage he can't yet see himself sucking dick. During overnighters in my king-size bed and in the buddy-buddy shower, Riley keeps me on my toes—and on my knees.

Riley's sexual aggression and me-first bad attitude are actually a major turn-on. If he only knew how much he resembles his hyper-sexed uncle who must have been hell-on-wheels at the same age. Riley and Ronny are both competitive team sport jocks with marathon physiques and attitudes to match. They're dark and not tall with lanky thighs, tight butt cheeks, and tireless boners. They both love to show off and strut their rowdy macho.

Riley admits that what attracts him most in other guys is "serious masculinity." He resembles his Uncle Ron most in this department. I'm also partial to alpha-masculine boys and masculine pursuits, so Riley and I have a lot in common from the get-go.

He tells me he likes older guys—mid-thirties is way-old to immortal young Turks like Riley. I'm pretty sure he's pulling my chain. I've been around the block. I've been out since I was sixteen, and I appreciate splendid youths flexing their sexy macho and sounding off, but I know better than to believe everything they say. I'm giving rowdy Riley a lot of space and watching him strut his stuff. But I've seen it all before, so I'm just going with the flow, rolling with the punches, and covering as many bases as I can. Riley's depending on me to be the big guy and let him be the big guy.

After a couple of months of this under-the-radar dalliance, I let Riley know that it's up to him to come out to his uncle—Mommy can wait until much later if that's what he decides—and that he's responsible to let Ron know that he's been boyfriending up-close-and-personal with Uncle's ex. Since he was the one who initiated things and got the ball rolling, he'll need to be the one to break the news and take all the credit.

I'm playing this hand I've been dealt carefully. That way I hopefully won't be getting too much flack for robbing the cradle or being the seducer or whatever, though I'm careful not to resort to these particular clichés in my sermon. Riley decides he's ready to make the leap and come out to his uncle, but just to Ronny for the time being, so that's what he does.

Of course, Ron is all over me about it right away. He's a wee bit hot under the collar and is feeling sort of hurt and left out of the picture. He's still feeling super-protective, which is understandable. The first thing he wants to know is have I fucked Riley's rowdy little butt? Of course I haven't, and on some level he knows for sure I wouldn't—at this stage—but he has to vent anyway and get it out of his system.

Ronny tells me if I fuck his nephew he'll gnaw my dick off and morph me into a sissy soprano, or words to that effect. I assure him that my ongoing whatever with precious Nephew has been almost avuncular, and that all that's gone down so far is me, nothing more than sleepovers and a little friendly head. As he knows from experience teenage boys need a lot of head. Riley deserves the best and I'm okay with providing it. And, that if the boot was on the other foot, incestuous hypotheticals notwithstanding, he'd be handling things the same way I am.

Hopefully, my easygoing boyfriendly mentoring and head-giving coaching and stunt double sort-of-uncling will inspire Riley to take the initiative and make a move on a likely prospect more his own age. Ronny knows from experience same as I do that that eventuality is destined to be the inevitable outcome of all these playful masculine preliminaries. When Ron finally realizes that Riley is the one who's going for it and that he's being coddled and protected and is obviously having a good time, he lightens up and backs off and doesn't rain on Riley's parade. He wants me to keep him posted (incognito) and tells Riley just to be careful and have fun. Riley is gratified that he appears to have his uncle's green light. It makes him feel way more comfortable samesexually and he starts expanding his repertoire of tricks, which is altogether another story.

Simultaneous with these epiphanies, my penny stock holdings in a South American gold mining property go ballistic when the claim proves-out and overnight I come into a tidy bundle. I sell off some stock and buy myself an ostentatious Hummer—don't ask me why. I also secure a timeshare in a condo at Whistler ski resort and buy the boyfriend a few toys to celebrate the windfall. I had heard Riley mention he was looking to replace his beater mountain bike. So we go power-shopping. He goes for the top-of-the-line XTR competition trail bike. I buy one for myself, too. A motorcycle is next on his list, and a new snowboard and boots, and while we're at it, a season pass for next winter at Whistler and Blackcomb mountains.

Riley acts like he deserves all this largess, which, of course, he does. He informs me that he also requires a leather jacket and Dayton boots to top off his edgy biker outfitting. He looks semi-tough strutting his stuff in his custom leather jacket.

Riley's still living at Mommy's house until he works up the nerve to come out to her and finally leave the nest. Right after his graduation, Ron had wrangled him a part-time job as a hardhat gopher at a downtown construction site. The temp gig lasted less than two months. Now he's got lots of free time on his hands.

I give him a key to my place and one to the condo up at Whistler, and things get all warm and cozy, and the boy starts sleeping over more often. To allay suspicions, Mom gets told that Uncle countersigned a loan for the new BMW street racer, and Ron's cabin in the Gulf Islands provides a likely alibi for all the overnighters.

In mid-August it's necessary for me to make a quick run up the Sea-To-Sky Highway to Whistler Mountain to tidy up some loose ends at the timeshare condo. I'd been wanting to put the big hulking Hummer through its paces and see how it rocks and rolls so I gas it up and aim it uphill.

It's a brilliant blue sky day in the mountains. It's hot and dry, and the summer season is at its peak. When I pull into the driveway in front of my rental condo I'm curious when I see Riley's new BMW two-wheeler parked on the pavement at the front door. The condo is locked and there is no sign of the boyfriend, though there's food in the fridge and a flat of empty beer cans in the recycling bin. The upstairs windows in the master bedroom are open and there's a couple of bath towels on the floor; the bed is a tangle of sheets, and there's a familiar pair of stylish tighty-whities hanging on the doorknob with a signature skidmark autographing the buttcrack. I figure Riley's up the mountain downhilling his new XTR trail bike.

I make a run to the town center to sign some paperwork at the realtor's, buy some groceries, and then muscle the Hummer back to the condo. When I re-enter the house there's a major surprise waiting for me. There are two mountain bikes in the entryway and a pair of naked hard-ons in the rec room. But luckily the third wheel isn't another man. It's a teenage boy.

Cool-As-A-Cucumber Riley caught with his pants down is unfazed. He doesn't miss a beat. He introduces his naked accomplice. The boy's name is Tanner. He's sixteen. He goes to the high school Riley just graduated from where he's next season's captain of the rugby squad. Tanner's a trophy-winning mountain bike scrambler, a competition team sport jock, and he's seriously cute and dangerous and obviously up for anything same as Mister Perfect.

Now that I've complicated things unexpectedly, Riley shifts gears and improvises. He cranks up the power and flexes his alpha-masculine testosterone to impress his rookie boon companion. He pops the tops off a couple of cans of beer and hands one across to underage Tanner. He condescends to ask me if I'd like one, too, hauls out a green bottle import out of the rec room fridge, pops the cap off and hands it across to me before I can answer yea or nay. Riley's being extra generous with his winner's largess. He got a royal flush on the deal and he's playing his hand all-in. The boy's on a roll. Riley's stylin'.

It looks like young Tanner got a royal flush on the deal, too—in spades. Tanner's a serious hunk. He's not tall and he's extra stocky. His humpy physique is well-upholstered all over. The boy is extremely good looking. He's dark and hyper-masculine and squeaky clean. Jet black buzzcut on top, bedroom eyes, and kissy lips. He's got a wide gap between his front teeth and a grin like a chipmunk. Short legs, massive thighs, and a great big butt. Tanner's got impressive masculine equipment. It's boned-out righteously and it looks like it works out a lot at the gym. It appears Riley has connoisseur taste in boyfriends. Tanner, of course, ditto.

Tanner stands in the center of the rec room, brandishing the TV clicker, radiating Olympian perfection and grinning like a chipmunk. Riley strikes a pornstar pose, guzzles his brew, and grins like a gold medal winner on the podium. I grin right back. I tell the bad boys that I'm hitting the showers. They need to find some clothes to climb into. We're heading out in the Hummer for fast food and a back road scramble up to a hidden mountain lake I know of for a late afternoon skinny-dip.

After junk food and an icy swim and an action flick in the town center, we hummer back to the condo after dark. The ah-ha moment occurs during a video war game in the rec room. It turns out that young Tanner is practically a local here at Whistler. His grandparents have a lakeside getaway at the north end of the valley, which Grandson has access to and dutiful responsibilities towards. It seems that popular Riley got himself included in several snowboarding weekenders at Tanner's mountain retreat during last winter's go-for-it season.

Riley informs me that he and Tanner intend to sleep three-way in the master bedroom instead of one-on-one in the guestroom. I figure Riley's wanting to show off to the new boyfriend; it turns out he wants to show off to me. In our big king-size bed, Riley showcases his freestyle head-giving technique working out on Tanner's muscle-bound masculinity. Riley's definitely taken it to the next level.

Come to find out Tanner likes playing strip poker, wrestling naked, and taking lots of showers same as Riley. The boys are a perfect match. Riley wants to know what I think of his new boyfriend. I tell him Tanner's a winner same as he is and they are both very lucky up-and-comers. He wants to know will I include Tanner in our ongoing masculine whatever here at Whistler next season and especially on whenever-overnighters at my avuncular hostelry down in the big city? I tell him he can count on it. Three's a charm.

Last Tango in Cambridge
Lewis DeSimone

I was twenty-two years old, and people were dying. That was my first excuse.

Maybe I just took to heart something that Bette Midler had once said. "I used to have indiscriminate sex," she opined, "but you can't do that anymore...You fuck the wrong person these days and your arm falls off."

I didn't want to lose an arm. Or anything else. Nathan had been in a monogamous relationship for five years, so he was safe. And as long as I slept only with him, I'd be safe, too. Physically, at least. Emotionally? Well, that's another story.

Besides, we were in love. That was my second excuse.

I'd never been in love before. In fact, falling in love with Nathan was what pulled me out of the closet.

We had been thrown together by circumstance (I'll leave it at that). He was older—smart and interesting, more worldly than I—a role model. I'd never had a gay friend before, and clearly that was part of my interest: Somehow, beneath all the denial, I knew he could help me. I just didn't know how.

We were sitting together on a swing in a friend's backyard, chatting quietly while everyone else gathered around the barbecue in the corner, stacking plates high with burgers and corn cobs. The light was growing dim, particularly in our little spot, under the cover of an oak tree.

We'd chatted like this many times before, Nathan and I. We'd known each other for nearly a year. I'd liked him instantly, but I wasn't aware of a physical attraction. In those days, I was seldom consciously aware of physical attraction to men.

I don't remember now what we were talking about that night, on the swing. He might have been telling me about the opera, or recommending a book, or relating some story about his travels. I don't remember the words. I remember his eyes.

Nathan's eyes were the color of lapis (a word I'd never heard at that point in my life, a word I've never used before this moment), the color of the bright patches dappling the ocean off the shore of Cancun (a sight I would not see for several more years). In those days, his eyes, to me, were just blue: pale blue, azure blue, bright and soft, liquid. And that evening—suddenly, in a moment that haunts me to this day—I fell into them. He laughed—the way he laughed, white teeth emerging beneath the heavy mustache so common among gay men of his generation. He laughed and his eyes grew brighter. And I knew. In an instant, as if someone had flipped a switch in my brain, I fell in love.

I'd spent half of high school and all of college in abject confusion—each crush on a boy followed immediately and oh-so-conveniently by a crush on a girl. I'd wondered for so long whether I was really gay, dreaming up rationalizations, that I didn't know which result to hope for. It was all hypothetical until this moment.

In an instant, in Nathan's eyes, everything became clear. In one epiphanic moment, the ancient question was answered, issue resolved, shame lifted. I no longer cared about the consequences of coming out—telling my parents, living the life of marginalization I expected in those pre-marriage, pre-military days. None of that mattered. It was all going to be easy now. I knew the truth, and the truth would set me free.

There was only one problem, one tiny little problem. As I gazed into Nathan's eyes, the joy in my heart suddenly plummeted. The problem wasn't that I was gay. The problem was that he was already taken.

But I was twenty-two. I was twenty-two, and naïve, and in love. And people were dying. I knew there was a whole world of gayness out there. It was Boston, not Missoula. I could have gone to bars, joined clubs, made friends.

But I was in love. It was too late for that. Nathan was all I thought I needed to know about love.

And that was my third excuse.

▲

NOW, WHEN I peruse my journal from those days, it's like reading a novel, but oddly backwards—every moment full of a weird kind of suspense because I know what's going to happen, but the author, the younger me, is clueless.

I danced around the situation at first, hinting to Nathan that I had a problem I wanted to discuss with him. He expressed interest, wanting to support me. But then he would back off, perhaps hoping that the problem, whatever it was, would just go away.

It didn't. There were moments when I thought it had gone away, when I could pass a night without thinking about him every minute and sobbing into my pillow. But then I would see him again, and the familiar rush of joy and agony would vibrate through me. I would go home at night and deepen the grooves in Carly Simon's *Torch* album, listening to her spill out my agony through melodic tales of love gone wrong.

If I'd had another gay friend to talk to, everything would have been different. Nathan might never have needed to know. But he was my only gay friend. In my mind at least, I had nowhere else to turn.

For me in those days, being gay wasn't an end in itself: It was a means to finding love. It was years before I would learn the simplicity of casual sex, before I was happy enough with my own company to appreciate a one-night stand or what one of my friends (yes, I eventually had gay friends) liked to call a "throw-down."

I already had the love. I had reached the goal. Why reverse course and start from the beginning—a beginning I'd been spared by fate? I had scored a touchdown before the kick-off, won a Pulitzer before writing a word. Who needed process?

Nathan saw it coming. Well, half of it, anyway. We hear what we want to hear. We hear as much as we can handle, and no more. He was expecting me to come out to him, to seek the advice of an older man, an experienced man—advice on what to do, how to be, now that I knew who I was.

But that's not what I asked. I didn't really *ask* anything at all.

"I realized something," I told him. I paused, forcing myself. In those days, I still had to force myself to express my feelings. "I'm in love with you."

I don't remember his response. My head was still swirling with my own words, my heart pounding, my entire body going numb with the strain of exposure.

When I awoke from the trance of having spilled my guts, he was talking about literature. The names spilled from him like water out of a leaky cup: Mary Renault, Christopher Isherwood, E.M. Forster. He gave me a reading list. Nathan was an intellectual—that was one of the things I loved about him. I confessed my love, and he gave me a syllabus.

▲

READER, I SEDUCED him. There's no way around the admission. I had a twenty-two-year-old one-track mind and a twenty-two-year-old bubble butt, which I crammed into tight jeans and a pair of shorts that would now barely make it around one of my middle-aged thighs. There's a photo of me in those shorts, playing volleyball on a group outing. They couldn't have been comfortable. Clearly, I was wearing them for one reason, and one reason only: to make Nathan drool.

It worked. It all worked—the hot pants, the flirtatious remarks. I was surprised to learn what a good flirt I could be, how easily the words flowed, words to describe things I had never even done yet.

I watched him for signs of desire—the way his eyes moved along my silhouette, the way words came stammering forth when my hand brushed against his in the middle of a story.

I was shameless. Looking back now, I'm ashamed of my shamelessness. And yet, he made it so easy. He didn't stop me. He didn't dare.

I pressed him. And finally, over a gin and tonic one evening, he admitted his attraction to me. The back-and-forth nature of the flirtation had not been my imagination. It was only a matter of time.

And one night, opportunity knocked. Nathan and I had plans with friends. We were going on an excursion to the Hancock Tower, to get a birdseye view of the city, but everyone else canceled. And so, there we were—Nathan and I at the top of the world, the observation deck of a building notorious for spitting its windows onto the street in rough winds, with an evening alone and nothing to do.

After taking in the view, we took in a cocktail at the hotel bar next door. And with no one to keep the subject on architecture, the flirting began. The conversation grew hot, innuendo giving way to explicitness. But still, it was all play.

Until the first kiss. Everything changed with the first kiss. That kiss drove me into his arms, drove him into my bed.

We did it on impulse. I suppose it couldn't have happened any other way. It had to be spontaneous, rushed, dangerous. We would never have done it otherwise, as long as we had time for words and regret and guilt. We couldn't have made that first move if it had been only about love. It had to be about sex, in its rawest form, in order to overcome our inhibition. It wasn't sex we were afraid of; it was love.

Getting physically naked together somehow made it easier

to be emotionally naked. In bed, gazing into my eyes, touching me, Nathan became more vulnerable to his own feelings. Denial fell away in the face of intimacy. While he may have been able to tell himself before that it was just an innocent flirtation, just a physical attraction, once we had sex, everything changed. I had fallen in love with him before we'd even touched. For me, sex was the physical culmination of an emotional state. For Nathan, it was just the opposite. He was first attracted to me physically, not romantically. But once our relationship became physical, he fell just as hard.

Our rendezvous became a semi-regular thing. Once a week, for longer than I care to admit, he would come over to my apartment on his way home from work, usually on nights when his partner was busy or working late. He was surprised, he said one night in my arms, to learn it was possible to love two people at once.

Apparently, quantity wasn't a moral issue for Nathan. Once he had cheated, there was no point in counting the times. He had already committed the sin; doing it again compounded nothing.

In the beginning, I wrote in my journal every time he left my apartment. I wrote painstaking descriptions of his body— the large nipples surrounded by curly brown hairs, the meaty thighs, the soft pink skin. I described in excruciating detail everything we did—the way his hands caressed my side, how smoothly our bodies coiled into position, the taste of his sweat on my tongue. I wrote about each meeting, compelled to get it all down, as if the words were all I had, as if I were afraid it would never happen again.

And when he wasn't there, when I craved his body, his lips on mine, my head on his chest—when I thought of him at home, across town, lying beside someone else—I fell to the floor of my studio apartment. I fell to the floor in tears, in physical pain. I fell to the floor and wondered if I would ever get up.

▲

I'D LIKE TO say I couldn't help myself, that Nathan was my drug of choice and therefore I *had* no choice. Isn't that step one, admitting you're powerless over your addiction? I'd like to say that, but it would just be another excuse. The truth is that I knew what I was doing. I wasn't so naïve as to believe that he would leave his partner for me, and I wasn't so oblivious as to believe that our affair was innocent. But I was romantic enough—and impassioned enough—to believe that none of that mattered. "Love is stronger than ethics," I wrote in my journal one night. It could have been my motto in those days.

I guess the deeper truth is that I bought into the romance. I may have known instinctively that my first lover wouldn't be my last, that even if Nathan were single, I would eventually leave him. But I'd read too many novels. Even when Madame Bovary was swallowing the poison, I was rooting for her. I understood why she did it. And, my head full of stories like that, I told myself that great love requires great pain. If I'd had a functional relationship back then, I wouldn't have known what to do with it.

Our time together consisted mostly of early evenings, in the middle of the week. Typically, he would stop by my apartment after work and we would build up an appetite, then go to dinner somewhere discreet. We were particularly fond of a small Indian place in Central Square, where the spicy food could distract me from the fact that I would soon walk him to the subway and return to an empty apartment.

He taught me about Indian food—how to cup the cubes of meat inside a torn-off piece of naan, how to relieve the heat with rice instead of water, which only spread it around your mouth rather than absorbing and washing it away.

Nathan opened me up to an entire world that even an Ivy League education hadn't taught me about. He gave me homework assignments—film and book recommendations, things to keep me busy on the nights when we weren't together. He gave me recordings of complete operas, and I would lie on my bed for hours at a time, following along with the translated librettos, tearing up when Rodolfo cried out Mimi's name for the last time, when the Marschallin said an inevitable farewell to her young lover. With the music swirling romantically around me, I could still feel Nathan's presence. It was as if Puccini and Strauss were a musical Cyrano de Bergerac, making a case for the tongue-tied lover.

▲

YOU'LL NOTICE THAT I haven't given you many details. Even now, I can't tell you much about him: his real name, where we met, what he did for a living—anything that might come too close to identifying him. Even now, all these years after I last laid eyes on him, I'm protecting his privacy. Even now, when, for all I know, he's already told his husband (I imagine them married now, first in line when Massachusetts made it legal) the entire story.

We were in love—I think I can safely say that. But "in love" probably didn't mean the same thing to both of us. Several years later, when I'd passed the age he was when we'd met, even I had a different definition for *love*. By then, I had had a few boyfriends. By then, my heart had been broken more than once, and I had broken a few others in return. And by then I knew that I would never again feel what I'd felt for Nathan—not because no one else would ever be as good as Nathan, but because no one else would ever be the first.

I wonder if a piece of me knew even then that the intensity I felt for Nathan would never come again. Perhaps that was why I couldn't let him go, despite the fact that our relationship was hopeless, that it could never be complete.

In hindsight, it's easy to see that the lack of fulfillment was ironically what kept us together. We enjoyed a perpetual romance—always tantalizing, always safely a fantasy. We never spent enough time together to truly grow tired of each other. We never had the chance to argue over housework or bills. He never dragged me along to family gatherings, never introduced me to "best friends" I couldn't stand. We met each week in a bubble. Our life together took place primarily in my studio apartment, in my twin bed. Despite the occasional excursion to dinner or a movie, our relationship ultimately took place in bed.

In the end, we didn't have time for love: time to sit quietly side by side in front of the TV; time to shop for Christmas ornaments; time to brush against each other in the kitchen, sharing steps in a recipe. Our moments together were few and short. We had to pack them with intensity. We packed them with sex. Sex was shorthand for all the rest.

▲

IT DIDN'T END the way it had begun, with the passion of spontaneity. It didn't end like a romance novel, the two of us riding off into the sunset on a white horse; or with drama—Nathan's partner bursting into the room as we writhed together on the bed. It didn't end with tragic inevitability: Nathan was no Anna Karenina, and I was no Vronsky; there were no fateful trains in our story.

But end it did. That much, at least, was inevitable. The relationship ended because I outgrew it, because the point came when I had to admit that it wasn't enough and would never be enough. It ended when I realized that my life had been on hold for too long.

I was still obsessed with AIDS—terrified and angry. And finally I chose to do something about it. I started volunteering at a local AIDS service organization—just administrative work, no sitting at bedsides or protesting in the streets, but the change was enormous for me nonetheless.

And finally, I made friends—friends I didn't have to come out to, or decide not to come out to, friends I didn't have to hide anything from. It became easy. A date, a kiss, a fun flirtation. And suddenly my life opened up before me, a life much bigger than the one I had shared secretly with Nathan.

THE LAST TIME WE spoke, Boris Yeltsin was standing on top of a tank. I was watching it on television, a revolution in progress. The world was changing in front of my eyes. Everywhere I looked, things were beginning. And ending.

At least that's how I remember the moment. I suppose it's not surprising that I've conflated those images in my head—the end of an empire, the end of a relationship.

My journal tells a different story. Our last conversation occurred during another summer, when I came home from graduate school, to visit my parents and help them pack. They had wanted to move to Florida for years, but only now were getting around to it.

I knew that my visits to Boston were likely to be few and far-between after my parents had left. This, I thought, might be my last chance to see Nathan. So I picked up the phone and called.

Surprised isn't quite the word to describe how he sounded when he recognized my voice. *Terrified*, perhaps? You'd think he was an illegal alien, and I an official from the INS. We made small talk for a while—stilted, but civil. Until I asked if he would be free for lunch while I was in town.

He hesitated. I suspected that he was debating whether to make an excuse or simply tell me the truth.

Evidently, he decided on the truth. "I don't want to open old wounds," he said. "That was one of the most painful periods in my life." He might have been reporting the weather.

He couldn't see me, he said, and then seemed to breathe a sigh of relief. He tried to resume the small talk, but I was having none of it. My stomach was churning. All I wanted was to get off the phone.

But as we were hanging up, he said it, one last time: "I love you."

In a novel, this scene would be considered an anticlimax. In life, if not in literature, I didn't know when to stop.

▲

THAT SAME SUMMER, I learned that a close friend from college had died of AIDS. One of my first thoughts, after the shock, the grief, was this: Nathan saved my life. If he hadn't come along, God knows what I might have done at twenty-two, a horny virgin in the middle of a plague.

One night not long ago, I thought I saw Nathan. A few rows ahead of me in a theater, I spotted the swoop of hair, the familiar shape of his nose in three-quarter profile. My heart raced for a moment, excited by the possibility of seeing him again, talking to him again.

It didn't take long to notice that the hair was still unmarred by gray, the skin too smooth—like my memories, untouched by time. Before the house lights went down and the show began, my reverie had ended. And I felt oddly relieved. The truth was that, beyond *hello*, I couldn't imagine the conversation, the feeble attempt to piece together the intervening years of our lives. I realized that I didn't want to know what he'd been up to since we'd last spoken. I didn't want to know how he'd changed, or hadn't changed. You can't go home again. Memory Lane is too full of potholes.

▲

SO THE PAST is the past, but I get to select the memories that are most important. I try not to remember the Nathan of that last conversation, with or without the tanks rolling through Red Square. I prefer to remember him in other moments—images that still linger in my mind: Our first stolen weekend together, when he taught me to make pasta Bolognese. He left the kitchen for a moment, to put some appropriate music on—Puccini, perhaps, our favorite—while I remained at the stove, stirring, drinking in the sweet tomato aroma. And suddenly he was behind me, his arms enfolding my waist, his chin resting on my shoulder. Or later that same weekend, when I was feeling particularly vulnerable, alone even in his presence because all I could do was imagine the lonely future. I climbed into bed, afraid to even ask him to hold me. And a moment later, he came to me in the darkness, his naked body a silhouette against the moonlight, kneeling on the bed, welcoming me into his arms.

I prefer to think of him like that, in the haze of romance. Even though I know better, I want him to stay like that—like a creature caught in amber, something beautiful I can pick up now and then, frozen, still, forever slightly unreal. I've had relationships since that started with just as much romance, but morphed eventually into imperfect reality. Let this one, I tell myself in moments like this, when I reach across the years, let this one be preserved the way it felt back then, when miracles still seemed possible, when romance would never end.

You Without Me
William Henderson

I GRAB YOUR face with both of my hands and pull your mouth to mine. Our mouths fit well, as do our bodies. I taste wine and chocolate. The candles you have lit smell like sandalwood. We are in your bed, on our sides, facing each other. You roll onto your back and pull me with you so that I am on top of you. We are kissing again. Kissing still. I stop kissing your mouth and I kiss your cheeks and your chin and your neck and I suck at your neck and your Adam's apple and I kiss your chest and bite your nipples and I kiss the scars on your forearms. The scars are uneven; one is darker and thicker than the other.

My arms are around you. I am scratching your back. You are moaning. I feel your vertebrae, the way your spine curves under your skin. I move one hand to the top of your shaved head and scrape my fingernails down from the crown of your head to the base of your neck. I can tell you like it. You kiss me harder and unbutton and unzip my pants.

When I come, I ask you to kiss me, and you do, and I know you can feel my orgasm through my tongue. You come, but do not ask me to kiss you.

I'm going to go clean up, you say, and you leave me in your bedroom. I think you want me to get ready to leave. The gray tank top you wore earlier is on the floor. I pick it up, smell it, and put in my pants pocket. My pocket bulges, so I put on my coat.

I have forgotten your name, though you told me yesterday. We met online, talked for a few days, and made plans to see each other. Last night, you jerked yourself off while our computers were connected via a video stream. I had asked you to do it to see if you would.

We planned to do more than separately masturbate tonight. We would drink wine, have sex, and, if we both felt like it, I would piss on you. But in that moment before our first kiss, I knew that we weren't going to fuck, and there certainly would not be any pissing.

I brought wine and chocolate, because you asked me to. I do not usually drink wine, because I do not think I really like wine. After tonight, I think I may like wine.

After tonight, I think I am ready to begin getting ready to admit to my wife of nearly a dozen years that I am gay and no longer interested in being married to her. We should get divorced, I will say. We should live close enough that we could easily share custody of our son.

You don't know about my wife, and I don't want you to know about her. I don't think you need to know about her.

I want to see you again, I said.

I want to see you again, too, you said.

I thought you might be saying it just to make sure you got off. But I kissed you anyway. I wanted to know what kissing you tasted and felt like. Your mouth did not feel strange. You, in that moment, and the moments that followed, did not feel strange.

You do not tell me that you are stoned, and I cannot tell that you are stoned.

I hear you coming back from the bathroom. I am dressed and ready to leave. I expect you to say thank you for coming and have a good night. You walk in.

I thought you might stay the night, you say.

I can't, I say. How late it's gotten.

You walk me to your front door.

I'll talk to you soon, you say.

I'm counting on it, I say. You kiss me goodbye. The kiss feels familiar and comfortable. I pull away. Goodbye, White Rabbit, I say.

You smile.

When can I see you again? I ask four days later. We have talked some since our first date, mostly by text message, and by text message I am asking to see you again. Are you still interested in seeing me?

Yes. You will have to officially ask me out, you say.

Do you want to go out with me? I ask.

Yes.

We make plans for Friday, three days from now. I wish we were getting together sooner. I wonder if we will fuck, or if we are still somewhere between second and third base.

On the night of my second date with you, I bring back the tank top I stole. My wife washed the tank top and asked me where it came from.

I've had it for a while, I say.

She didn't believe me, but didn't ask about it further.

I took home your tank top accidentally, I tell you. Must have gotten jumbled in my sweater.

You tell me on a different night that you knew I took home your tank top on purpose, and you were glad I took home your tank top on purpose.

Want to get sushi? you ask.

I offer to drive us to the restaurant. I don't think about my son's car seat until I open the passenger-side door for you. You do not look in the backseat. I do not know that you are more stoned than you were on our first date. I still do not know that you were stoned on our first date.

My car is stuck in the snow and ice in your driveway. We manage to free the car, but I do not want to risk getting stuck somewhere else. The sushi restaurant is close, so we decide to walk.

Will I see you again next Friday? I ask.

Yes, you say. If you want to.

Yes. That's less than 168 hours from this moment in time.

How did you figure that out so quickly?

I laugh. Twenty-four hours in a day, seven days in a week. Multiplication.

While walking to the restaurant, you ask me to be quiet.

Why? I ask.

Can't you hear it?

And I listen. I don't hear anything, and then you say, there, crunch.

What? I ask.

The snow and ice under our feet, as we walk, crunch, you say.

And you walk a few feet, and I can hear the sound you're talking about; the sound sounds like a crunch. Your eyes shine. I recognize this look. My son gets the same look when he says a word for the first time, or when he is able to make himself understood.

We order our sushi. Instead of waiting in the restaurant, you ask if I want to take a walk, and we walk to the courthouse in the small town where you live. Christmas lights still hang on storefronts and on houses.

I have something to say, you say.

The way you say I have something to say drains the night of any possibility I thought it held.

I'm a former crystal meth addict.

The other shoe, dropping. I've been waiting for it. Never mind my marriage. That is not the other shoe. I can get out of it. I want to get out of it. I have been afraid to get out of it. I'm not even sure I will tell you about my marriage. Why would you want to have sex with someone—let alone date someone—who is married, albeit unhappily?

You continue talking. I haven't used in a while, but when I use, nothing else matters. And the last time I used, I destroyed my life, hurt people I loved, and almost died. Crystal left me with nothing, and I know if I use again, I will not come back. I will use until I die.

But you don't use now, I say, like I am asking, not telling.

No, but I like to occasionally get high. I only recently started smoking. I never buy it. My roommate gives it to me.

You shaved your head before I came over. I focus on it, and on your eyes, and on the way you look afraid of my response. I can't see your mouth. Your scarf covers it.

I don't know what we're becoming, you say, but if we're becoming anything, if you ever think that I may possibly use crystal, or if you think my drug use is growing out of control, then you have to promise that you will do whatever it takes to stop me.

Then you unwrap your scarf and tie it around my neck.

Yes, I say, because I don't know what else to say. Yes, I promise I will do whatever stopping you takes.

You smile. I like your smile. I like your mouth, the way it is mostly even, but slightly not, and the way it feels against mine. Felt against mine. You and I haven't kissed tonight. Maybe we won't kiss. Maybe what we're becoming won't involve kissing.

We should get back, you say, and I want you to hold my hand, but you don't, and I'm not brave enough to reach for your hand. I want you to hold my hand because I want to focus on that and not on what you've just told me.

While I am mulling your admission of being a drug addict, or a former drug addict, I enjoy the fact that you pay for our sushi. Yes, I may have been the one to ask you out, but you're taking me out. A beautiful man with a British accent—for you went to boarding school in England and picked up a British accent while you were there—is taking me out on a date.

I do not think about my wife and son asleep in our home. They are not part of this life where I am eating sushi at nearly eleven P.M. with a man they know nothing about. You are mine, I think. This, right here, right now, what I'm feeling, all mine.

When we get back to your apartment with our sushi, you set the table. We use real chopsticks, not the disposable kind that comes with takeaway. You feed me what you are eating.

I like you, you say.

I like you, too, I say.

No, I mean I really like you.

You stop talking, as if embarrassed.

I really like you, too, I think. I have not felt this kind of liking in more than a dozen years. I like feeling this kind of liking.

We finish dinner and decide to watch a movie. I get into your bed. You lean your head into my shoulder. You fall asleep before the movie ends. I wait until the credits roll, get out of your bed, put on my shoes, turn off your computer, and blow out candles you lit before we started watching the movie.

We didn't have sex. We didn't kiss. But what we did feels more intimate than if we had had sex or if we had kissed.

What time did you leave, you ask me the next day.

After the movie ended, I say.

The next night, I text to see if I can return a book I borrowed and get the next book in the series. I don't have to come in, I write. I'll stand outside and jump in the snow so that it crunches, and you can open a window and toss me the book. Or, if you want, I can hold a boom box over my head and play Peter Gabriel for you.

Even then, not yet ten days into our relationship, I wanted to skip ahead to the end of the movie. Give me my romantic ending. Give me the over-the-top moment when you realized that life without me was worse than life with me. No matter that I don't have a boom box and had no idea where I could get one. You didn't get the reference to *Say Anything*.

Of course you can come over, you say.

Of course I can come over.

You worked all day. You are in human resources at a retail store. A customer complained about an employee. You tell me the story. You know you will have to take care of the complaint. Your bong is on your desk.

I didn't smoke much before you got here, you say. Do you want to smoke some?

No, I say. I take off my shoes and get in your bed.

I watch you smoke. One hit. Two hits. Three. I watch your exhalation. Part of me wants to ask for some, but part of me knows that I don't like weed, and I especially don't like not feeling in control.

Do you want to hook up? I ask.

Okay, you say. I know that's why you really came over.

Maybe hooking up is why I really came over.

You straddle my body and begin to kiss me. You taste like pot. I haven't tasted pot in several years, and only then because my wife and I, in an attempt to recapture what we had in college, got high.

You get off of the bed and you pull off my jeans and you pull down my briefs. You suck me off until I come, and as I feel it building, I warn you. I expect you to stop and finish me off in your hand, but you don't, and when I am done, I push you onto your back and do the same to you. I do not like the taste of come.

You to me, the next day, via a text message: I like you, and I can't stop thinking about you, and I wonder if you would like to date it out.

What does that mean? I ask.

I want to see where we are going. I want to see where this is going. Do you want to find out, too?

Yes, I say.

Do you want to be in a monogamous relationship with me?

Yes. We've seen each other three times in ten days.

You need to say the words, well, type them.

Which I do.

I want to be in a monogamous relationship with you, I type.

I'm glad, you say. Can you come over during the week?

We make plans. You call me your boyfriend. I tell you I need to sleep.

▲

TWO MONTHS GO by, during which time I continue hiding my marriage. The afternoon of my birthday, we take long lunch breaks and meet at your apartment. Before we eat lunch, we make love, and it is good and tender, which is one way we do it. I like that we make love along a continuum. Sometimes you handcuff my hands above my head, push me against a wall, and suck me off until I come, not letting me touch you or move much. Sometimes in your bed you straddle me and lower yourself onto me. Other times, you are on your back, or on your knees, or we are on the floor. Or we fuck in the shower, standing up. Once, we started in the shower, but you wanted it deeper, so you got out, kneeled, and we finished on the bathmat; the water ran the entire time.

I go to the bathroom when we are done, and when I come out, you are putting sashimi on plates. I lean into your back and wrap my arms around you. You stop what you are doing.

There's something for you on the table, you say.

I pull away and look at the table. There is a small red box. Not much could fit in the box. The box was not here before.

Do you want me to open the box now? I ask.

Yes, you say.

There is a note on top of a layer of cotton: *Wear me.* I put the note aside. I lift the cotton, and underneath is the key you have been wearing. I hadn't noticed that it wasn't around your neck. You've been wearing the key around your neck for a few weeks. The key opened your childhood bedroom door, you've told me. The key is on a chain. The key is magic.

Really? I ask.

You walk over and you pick up the key and you clasp the chain around my neck.

I love it, I say.

I hope so, you say. You'll be wearing it forever.

Okay, I say. I can do that.

No, you say, you don't understand. When we get married, I want to melt the key and use it to make your ring. You will wear my past on your finger as a symbol of our future and life together.

Our bands won't match, I say.

I don't care, you say. I want you to have my past. I want you to have my future. You have it all, Rabbit. You know that.

So are we engaged? I ask. We have been together about ten weeks. I want you to want to marry me because I want to marry you. I love you—that should be enough.

Not yet, you say. I'll let you know.

I decide to propose to you about four months later. After work, I come to your apartment. I've had keys to your apartment for a couple of months. I let myself in and walk into your bedroom.

You still don't know about my wife, and I still don't know how to tell you about my wife, and I still don't know how to tell her about you, and I still don't know what to do about all of the things I don't know.

She and I are going away for the weekend. We're taking our son. Of course we're taking our son. I told you I was going away for a work thing. You asked me if you could come. I told you that my work thing was not the kind of thing where plus-ones are invited.

Hi, I say, crawling in next to you. I lean into you and kiss you.

I'm going to miss you, Rabbit, you say. You wrap your arms around me. I don't like when you go away.

I'm never far, I say, and I kiss you. I reach into my pocket, pull out the ring, and put it on your finger. The ring does not fit. You turn your hand upside down. The ring slides off. You look at it and then at me.

It doesn't fit, I say. I'm sorry.

Rabbit, you say, and you stop talking.

You are crying. You look at the ring, and then you kiss me.

I can get it re-sized, I say.

I love it, you whisper. I love you.

You unhook the necklace you are wearing, put the ring on the chain, and re-clasp the necklace around your neck.

Will you marry me? I ask, and when I ask I feel like I've

never meant anything more than I do in this moment, asking you to promise me forever, because with you, forever doesn't even seem long enough.

Your voice cracks when you say, yes.

I'm sorry it doesn't fit, I say.

It's perfect.

On my way home, I text that I want to spend the next fifty-seven years with you. I want to wake up next to you, and go to bed next to you, and take care of you, I text. I want to see the life our children will have. I want adventures, and I want to travel. There will be hard days, and there may come times when we want nothing more than to walk away. But I promise you that I will always come back. I believe in us. I believe in you.

You know you will have to tell me all of this in person, you reply. I will not settle for a text-message proposal. I won't even settle for a bedroom proposal while we are in bed. I want you there, on one knee, and I want to see you cry. I want it in public and messy. I don't want you to ask me safely. I want to know that you mean forever when you ask me for forever. And when I say, yes, and I am definitely saying, yes, then you will know that I mean forever and that no one else will do. I want to look into your eyes when you are proposing, and I want you to look into mine when I say, yes.

Does this mean we're not engaged? I ask.

No, Rabbit, you text. I love you, and I want to marry you. We're engaged.

⁂

OUR ENGAGEMENT LASTS less than a month. You begin smoking an ounce of marijuana every three days. You no longer accept marijuana from your roommate in lieu of payment for bills. You begin buying from him, and, in return, you begin selling to your best friend.

I never meant to deal, you tell me.

So stop, I say.

But you can't stop, and I know you can't stop, and even though you don't tell me you can't stop, I know you can't stop, and I know I can't stop you. How can I stop you? I didn't even know how to begin you, and then there you were, and there we were, and I look around your bedroom and I no longer can tell where you end and I begin, and where I end and you begin, and I don't want to find that fault line separating us though I know the fault line is growing and cracking and some days I can feel the earth shaking under our feet.

We are fucking two and three times a day. We fuck to keep from talking. Or I fuck to keep from talking. I don't want to say anything I will regret, though I keep thinking things that I regret. How can I marry a man who uses? How can I trust a man who uses? How can you be happy with a man who won't use with you?

To keep you from using, I start bringing over bottles of wine, and on the nights when you and I finish a bottle, or sometimes two, you don't use. Somehow, drinking and getting drunk and having sloppy sex and sometimes fighting with you over silly things like which movie to watch and whose turn it is to bottom seems better than watching you get high.

I pull away, and you can tell I am pulling away, and you ask me what is wrong, and I tell you nothing is wrong, but I want to tell you that everything is wrong, and I'm glad the ring doesn't fit because I no longer want you to have the ring, and I have never broken an engagement before and I still don't want to see me without you, but really, if I'm being honest, and what else can I be but honest, I am already me without you. I just refuse to see you without me.

AND THEN THERE WAS ONE
RODNEY ROSS

WE ARE THE Other Couple.

It's not what you think.

Look elsewhere for a *ménage a quatre*.

This isn't *Bob & Floral & Ted & Phallus*.

We're the college sweethearts who surprised even ourselves by prevailing, at this writing, thirty years. Our physiology must self-manufacture Gold Bond Powder, because we've skipped over the seven-year itch four times plus. Truthfully, that we are The Other Couple isn't so special. There's nothing to mythologize here. We simply lasted. Plentiful are our own missteps, but they will not be articulated in this essay collection; it can, however, be revealed that none were ever grounded in The Other Man.

The Other Loan, The Other Job, The Other Nightcap, The Other Mother, maybe.

We're old school. I have access to his Internet passwords. He's used my toothbrush in a pinch. Oh, we'll pick at each other's scabs, but we never draw blood.

Fossils?

Possibly.

I've heard a rumor that in the proposed plotline for the next *Jurassic Park* sequel, scientists will attempt to replicate us.

That we have demonstrated the survivalist instincts of Cher seems to have increased our go-to value. Couples gravitationally tend toward the easy shorthand of other couples and we're no exception. We become Agony Aunts to younger associates, trying not to be too world-weary or jaded with our anecdotes and advice; we function as dinner guest buffers between squabbling M/M couples older than we, who make Martha and George look like a warm-up act; among peers around our age, between caftan and catheter, we talk about the importance of a king-sized bed.

Three decades have witnessed too many dissolutions to count. To enumerate them I'd need your fingers, the fingers of the person you lend this book to, plus all toes (but only if you've recently been to the spa for a pedicure.)

It was no more our intention to become The Other Couple than it's someone's objective to be water boarded.

Both share much in common.

Inevitably, break-ups became grisly audience participation, a reality show where someone gets voted off.

The painful, protracted break-ups, they're the worst. The division of Tommy Bahama, once shared, to separate closets. Angry outbursts over house pet custody, then the sad realization that neither really wants the responsibility. Barter over vacation scrapbooks and holiday keepsakes: "I'll trade you Maui for the Grinch cookie jar." Dinner guest lists have to be redrawn to exclude the offending party and discreet surveillance is occasionally conducted on behalf of the wronged party—this is the person who best convinces you he has been wronged, although occasionally you will be deceived or your own instincts will misdirect you.

It may not be explicitly verbalized, but you will always be expected to choose. One general takeaway: At the first inkling of a split in the offing, tread cautiously.

Do not make a propellant noise with your lips and declare, "I never liked him anyway!"

For the love of God, do not, DO NOT, demonstrate solidarity by finding a razor blade and gleefully decapitating the ex in a group photo.

This will be dredged up should they reconcile. You will be marked as disloyal, quick to leap.

Take this as a hypothetical cautionary tale.

Neither of us ever did this.

Really.

▲

ALEX AND TOM were clearly unsuited. Alex had calculated his own, then Tom's, body fat and would determine their food portions. We saw him once slap Tom's hand when reaching for the breadbasket. Tom was no prize. He kept a photograph of a fake fiancée on his desk at the Fortune 500 company he worked for and he'd even named her Chelsea. Spending time with them started giving us headaches. Sifting their contradictory statements made us feel we were a two-person jury sequestered *forever.*

A couple that didn't cohabit, they should have. Sharing an address might have tempered the self-loathing and quelled some of the suspicion. It became quite the CGI special effects show as trust and control issues morphed into irritable resentment and pixilated into 24/7 paranoia. After two A.M. one night, Tom investigated the sound of a raccoon in the garbage. He found Alex in the alley, a penlight between his teeth, sifting his refuse for telltale signs of cheating: a used condom, a credit card receipt from a place they'd never been, a hoop earring someone had left tangled in the sheets. He mumbled something about designer sunglasses that might've been trashed, but the jig was up. Some phantom mediator gave us custody of Tom who, as it turned out, *was* a serial cheater. He had so many chat room and message board nom de plumes it was a miracle he remembered how to endorse a check.

▲

FOR RANDY, NO relationship lasted longer than a rinse cycle.

"You guys are still together. Why can't I manage that?" he wailed. Randy was always the one cuckolded and he didn't understand why he wasn't impervious to infidelity. "I have great guns and size fourteen feet." We didn't tell him that believing those were the key to a happy household was his problem. We were too busy staring at his feet.

▲

WE UNDERSTOOD WHY a fairly new couple, Gerard and Mike, splintered. After over almost eighteen months together, Mike confessed a mind-blowing deception: He'd been positive for six years. No matter how empathetic you are, a sin of omission like this is pretty hard to handle.

"Is there anything else I need to know?" Gerard challenged Mike.

Yes, there was.

The vacant property next door, the one with the spectacular waterfront perspective?

Mike's retired mother, a faded Southern belle who recalled all of Tennessee William's women and liked her Percocet a little too much, had bought it. Construction would soon commence on the house of her dreams and of Gerard's nightmares.

That a complicated pharmaceutical regimen had been concealed and their sex life compromised was one thing.

HIV, Gerard said he could handle.

Violet Venable, an easement away?

That was the bigger no-no.

When Gerard moved out, he relocated in our kitchen. Not only did we provide emotional support, we provided nutritional sustenance, since he couldn't cook and proved it by setting fire to spaghetti, which we never could quite figure out. A newly-single friend can be an expensive proposition; we started buying three steaks, not two. When he gradually stopped appearing at our back door like a boxcar transient holding a fork and knife, we assumed he found a better Automat.

▲

WITH LUCIUS, WE made the mistake of counseling forgiveness. "Do I look like a Kennedy wife?" he demanded. "Take him back, hate myself, drink excessively?"

Choosing Absolut over absolution, Lucius began to drink excessively. After his third DWI, he lost his operator's license and was seen on a city bus, probably going across town to report to the new Other Man in his life: a probation officer.

▲

DARREN AND RYAN were different. Their relationship didn't have the longevity of ours but so much time spent together as a foursome made it seem so. Unapologetically clique-ish, we weathered crises and celebrated victories; we had prayed on turbulent flights and drove each other home from colonoscopies; we even donned one another's drag wigs. Now *that's* friendship.

But, as someone more erudite than I could have prophesied, shit happens.

Frequent, work-related travel to a corporate office on the West Coast bolstered not only Ryan's Dividend Miles but offered the bonus of a fling with an outside supplier. Ryan was wined, dined, and ultimately concubined.

If only Ryan had left the infatuation behind at the hotel, with the lemon-verbena shampoo.

"There was a misunderstanding about monogamy in our household" was Darren's initial, mysterious explanation of their domestic crisis.

No, a misunderstanding is about whose turn it was to empty the dishwasher.

You might break a coffee cup for dramatic effect, preferably one that you never cared for, with a logo, but you don't break up.

They broke up. All was revealed.

Before parting after one rendezvous, Ryan and the vendor had burnt each other a love ballad compilation CD. (I know. We groaned, too, especially when we caught wind that the line-up included "I Finally Found Someone" by Bryan Adams and Streisand.) It was this custom-designed jewel case insert, with hearts and treacly song titles, that was Ryan's undoing when Darren, being all husbandly and unpacking his carry-on, discovered it.

This lady-or-the-tiger was easy. Ryan maturely assumed responsibility for the fracture and stayed away. Darren came to weep on our shoulders so often we began draping a bar towel on them if we knew he was coming by.

"I'm the laceless tennis shoe you see on the shoulder of the highway," he sobbed.

If I didn't drown in his tears, I was going to drown in analogies. I excused myself to get a squeeze mop.

But he was heartbroken.

So, selfishly, were we.

They were like us.

Now they weren't.

We proceeded with sensitivity. Our shared lives went everywhere, *were* everywhere. We cleared shelves—and cupolas that only The Gay would tuck something into—of framed photographs in happier times and happier places like Bermuda, Provincetown, France. (This preceded Instagram. Now we'd just change our Facebook settings.) Not only did we not speak Ryan's name, we avoided words that rhymed with it. We even hid our deck of Old Maid.

This was not enough.

New rules of friendship were formulated by Darren and brutally enforced. When word got back from someone with an agenda that we exchanged pleasantries with the ex as we shopped zesters in a Williams-Sonoma, the ceiling fell in.

Relenting after several days of silence, Darren settled into a chair, crossed his arms so tightly he had deep cleavage, and demanded specifics. I pacified him with every syllable of the perfunctory conversation, but when he asked how Ryan looked and I off-handedly shrugged really good, the windows blew out.

I ran to check our homeowner's insurance to see if we had *Overreaction* coverage.

Being recast as a tripod led to momentary speculation—more flatter than slander—that *we* were The Other Men, shameless hussies who caused, or at least facilitated, Darren and Ryan's break-up. Nothing could be further from the truth. That very cozy table of four in our favorite tapas restaurant was now a very morose trio. If the empty chair wasn't enough, a hostess or server might blithely note, "You don't need this, do you?" and whisk it to another table. Sure, the sangria went further, but each plate usually bore small four bites—more reproach. Whoever finally took the uneaten prosciutto-wrapped date stuffed with goat cheese felt deceitful, like Ryan would return from the men's room any minute and we'd gobbled his portion.

We found a new favorite restaurant, a noodle place where we each got our own entrée.

When Ryan dumped the long-distance vendor and began essentially cohabiting with a local man a decade-plus his junior, things got particularly bad.

"What kind of CD will he make for his trophy wife? Barney sing-a-longs?" Darren spat.

He was especially dejected about his own prospects. Worthy boyfriends, much less life partners, are not spring-loaded, we reminded him. When one falls away, a suitable replacement does not automatically push forward. Until that far-off day when he caught the bride's bouquet again, he'd be just fine, we encouraged him, which demonstrated how near-sighted we were.

He grew fiercely competitive. Every waking moment was an opportunity to see or be seen. He ironed before he mowed, installed a mirror by the telephone, had floss in every drawer and his driving became erratic.

"These bare-chested joggers distract me," he giggled as his new red BMW convertible jumped onto the curb.

Everyone became his Dolly Levi. Dates weren't just blind, they came with black sunglasses. The lesbian ethos of moving too quickly had nothing on him. He'd leave the house with change-of-address cards in his glove compartment. When the Pez did not dispense Mr. Right, he embarked on a self-improvement regimen that did not extend itself to reading a book, working a crossword, or even just standing still and paying attention. He relied on a tanning bed, a dicey procedure called mesotherapy to chemically melt belly fat, and new sideburns as reasonable facsimiles of a personality.

We did our breathless best to keep pace with his new life, but his stride was considerably more caffeinated (which we found out later was actually coked). We accompanied him into bars and night clubs because he couldn't bear walking in alone. The few times he had, so many tongues clicked it was like he'd stumbled into a tap dance class, he claimed. When he sank several pool balls at first break, he bitched, "Even they're running away from me." Should Darren have found the face of Jesus in his beer foam, Our Lord would be looking over his shoulder for a better prospect. If an object of desire rebuffed his advance, he immediately wanted to "blow this joint. It stinks of rejection." Even if we were having fun, out we trotted, in cock-step with him.

One night, we were pressed against free wall space like a police ID lineup. The track lighting directly above had all red bulbs, leftover from Christmas, maybe, or Valentine's Day. We looked livid or embarrassed but certainly not approachable. My partner was then reading *Openly Bob*, stand-up comic Bob Smith's essay collection. He recounted something he found funny: how Bob, when he first and very anxiously ventured into gay bars, was told by a friend to relax his lower lip. His body, the theory went, would go into freefall with it and send out the right come-hither message. I took this a step further when an entreaty my grandmother would offer came to me. When something didn't turn out well, whether it was a mayonnaise jar lid that wouldn't yield or a home perm that didn't take, she'd advise:

"You didn't have your mouth just right. You've got to hold it a certain way."

If the eyes are the mirror into one's soul, a lot of people need Windex. Most of the auras we were getting a gander at in the bar resembled a neglected aquarium. So we lowered the bar and made a game of it, staring at the posture of mouths, amassing un-scientific data and, at the same time, collecting toothpicks from our many martinis.

We quickly spotted hopeful, chapped, lopsided, smug.

Frowning was bad and yawning was worse, we all agreed.

Darren announced one guy at the end of the bar had cat mouth, "that oddly-held mouth a cat gets when they get a whiff of something unfamiliar or repellent."

Many men were thin-lipped, like a lazy artist never inked in the two horizontal lines. The good news was, with no mouth at all, at least they couldn't open it and blow it. A counterfeit mouth, enhanced with filler or a temporary plumping serum, was just too fussy. If an absurdity didn't fall out of it, a silk and beaded purse would.

One especially ugly mouth was spewing such vitriol we were sure the teeth would perforate its own tongue. His mouth didn't even matter. This old coot in head-to-toe International Male just needed to hold his checkbook right.

I told them about a friend in the performing arts who, when a camera is present, presses his tongue hard against the back of his upper teeth. This, he explained, firmed the jawline and accentuated cheekbones, a facial callisthenic that worked as a temporary facelift. We all tried it, pretending that the carpet, not just our faces, was red, and that we were at an Oscar arrival photo op. I immediately got a neck cramp.

Restless, we began to slur call-outs.

"Fever blister."

"Hiding gumminess."

"Teeth whitened today."

"Struggling to contain drool."

"Constipated or piles."

"Holding a wobbly partial in place."

And then a friendly hand was extended from nowhere.

"You have great dimples!" Darren was being told.

The bookends that looked like they had really bad rosacea weren't such cockblocks after all. Woo was being pitched. Darren began to work his dimples like Sue Ann Nivens.

We made ourselves scarce in a vestibule, going from crimson to shadow.

Then, unexpectedly, green.

Right about now is a good time to address the by-product of this.

Darren had gotten in touch with his inner mouth. Clearly doing something very right with it, he transferred this savvy to other orifices. Things started to go his way. He would wax euphoric about hook-ups. We demanded salacious details, then got pissy when he told us. As much as we had bitched about his neediness, the affirmation he craved and we supplied in abundance, now he was blossoming. The Other Couple was jealous.

What a clumsy landing, to become The Smother Couple, resenting whoever next came to play in Darren's sandbox. And there were a lot of nexts, a lot of Other Men. Sweaty bodies were being thrown against the wall to see what stuck. Life became a cruise and the gangplank led into his bed.

We didn't count on envying his freedom, but we did. It was a little heady and it was his, not ours. Like a long-held POW, released, he went to work with his bed unmade, taboo in our house. He might kiss someone unexpectedly. His hair was foiled while ours betrayed gray, and he had his chest waxed because some twenty-two-year-old twink who had never chewed Freshen Up Gum had gone *eeeewwwww*. Darren was no longer the roadside sneaker. He, in fact, bought shoes with a trendy toe. A body-conscious wardrobe went perfectly with his new toes. Our wet noses were pressed against the store window of his full Fagmalion makeover, and we were wearing scuffed Skechers.

He subscribed to something called *Circuit Noize*, which I thought was a leaflet about either tinnitus or DIY instruction on electrical work. The implication was that circuit parties represented a bold and revolutionary family. A small and smudged font breathlessly listed when and where you could be adopted into a drug-addled reunion in white. If this was a family, where was Mom? I never found her in the pictures, but I saw a lot of simian jawlines, denizens from the *Planet of the Apes* make-up trailer, men so obviously juiced they must ejaculate in pill form. I began to worry Darren would end up like Tom Bianchi, but without the camera.

It wasn't worry.

It was a fresh surge of envy.

He didn't even tell us about a spontaneous trip to Vegas until, on his kitchen counter, we saw the Caesar's Palace change cup; it had a rose in it. Once we recovered from what he'd paid for airfare and a last-minute hotel room, one of us, I can't remember which, asked about the rose.

"It's from Louis," he said shyly, "my late-night fuck buddy." It didn't faze him that Louis was partnered and came over only when his boyfriend was away. "I'm doing nothing wrong," he replied tersely when we pointed out he was The Other Man. "He's the liar."

We automatically declined his invitations to go drinking during the work week. We couldn't bear seeing him exchange phone numbers or saliva. As we opted out, he stopped checking in. Then he stopped calling. Friendship became acquaintanceship.

He was spotted in a club, wearing only a red Speedo, doing The Twist, on a plywood cube, from which he later fell; we knew we had lost our foundling. The two of us had constituted one very big teat, but The Other Man who had come to nurse was sated and burped and was off to find not another titty but a pec. We heard from others his management job was considered redundant and how he was offered, and took, relocation to a state ending with an S. We waited for a bon voyage dinner to be hosted by all of his new bachelor friends, but there were just goodbye shots at a Levi/leather bar. We didn't go.

It started with a thoughtful birthday card to me, then we were making visors of our hands and catching up at a sunny outdoor art fair and that's how Ryan, Darren's ex, eased back into our radius. He was now with someone age-appropriate. He fully acknowledged the hurt he'd caused but didn't regret the distance he put between us.

"I figure Darren needed you more than I did," he said, not unkindly. "He always wanted us to be more like you two."

We looked at each other in wonderment. "How so?" Still a little bruised, we were ready for some uplift of our own.

"You're sturdy, you're never messy, you don't fall apart."

We sounded like an adult diaper. The only adjective missing was two-ply.

"Darren once said, 'If I was on Death Row and it was my last meal, I'd want to eat it with them.'" When our eyes bugged, Ryan added, "Guys, he meant it as a compliment."

▲

GOOD FRIENDS OF ours, Tom and Bradley, paired for seven years, have hit a rough patch, based on one's career trajectory and a sudden imbalance in incomes. Why one can't be elated by the other's success mystifies us, but that's beside the point. Like an agonizingly slow drag queen reveal, we've been getting flashes of what's under the sheath. We knew something was up when Tom confided he hid a Ghirardelli chocolate bar in the crisper under a head of lettuce.

"I'm tired of Fatass scarfing down my sweets," he groused.

The crystal balls do not lie: We are again going to be The

Other Couple.

"We're too old for this shit," we groan.

Yet we cling to the ideal that you're never too old to be receptive or susceptible to the vagaries of the human heart. My novel, *The Cool Part of His Pillow*, explored a man tragically thrust into becoming the Me of a We by a construction crane accident that kills his longtime partner. In no way autobiographical—although I cop to the occasional homicidal thought—the echoes of this fictional forty-five-year-old man's footfall gave me new insight. Our own relationship may not have an expiration date, but the vessel we dwell in sure as hell does. Someday, The Other Couple will become The Other Man, the last one standing, alone and lonely.

Tom and Bradley are confiding separately. We are told via text they've "temporarily" moved to separate bedrooms. A quick e-mail mentions a vacation apart to "sort things out." We even know about a secret Grindr account, which will cease being a secret when the other downloads the app.

I like Bradley better; my partner favors Tom.

I don't yet know who will be sitting at it, but, in my mind, I have already put a third plate on the dinner table.

THE CHILD
FELICE PICANO

WHEN IT BECAME clear that Bob Lowe was not going to make it, that his organs were shutting down, one after the other, and it was only a matter of minutes until intubation would occur, medically needed to keep him breathing, and therefore he'd be unable to talk, he called me over in private and we talked about final things, things important to him. These ranged from the serious, "Try not to hate Fafner too much!" (His name for his dragon of a mother) to the superficial, "Take my brand new Bill Robinson rayon/linen sports jacket made in Hong Kong out of my closet and put it in yours and make sure you wear it." To each, of course, I said sure, sure, of course. Even when he said, "Look after The Child." Even to that, I agreed, although under my breath I said, "Like *that's* going to happen!"

And so we completed what needed to be said, before the awfulness of that tube going down his throat began. I only left long after he'd fallen asleep when I was kicked out. I would never see him conscious again.

I kept all of those promises. I still have that jacket and I occasionally wear it, but the most difficult ones proved difficult indeed. And then there was the problem concerning The Child.

This name referred not to any actual child of ours, or of Bob's, but instead to a grown man, indeed an overgrown man, weighing close to two hundred-and-fifty pounds, who admittedly was younger than we were—we were in our mid-forties—but again not by that much.

He had come into our lives several years before as Bob's "other man" and then he'd left, but then it turned out he'd never really left at all.

⚑

WE'D BOTH HAD "other men" in our lives. Because we'd met in 1975, and in 1975 gay men did not get married, gay men did not adopt, gay men seldom purposely sired children. That was not what it meant to be a 60's/70's gay man rebelling. Not one bit.

Instead we had "open relationships," and although more than sixteen years had passed for us, people would see us somewhere and say in wonder, "Are you guys still together?" The truth was, yes, we were still together. One reason for that was we had had a so-called "open relationship" to begin with; that had removed a lot of unnecessary limits, strictures and, let's face it, a lot of pressure. The exact degree of openness had altered radically since 1975, and in the final decade our relationship had been open only a tiny bit.

But because we were friends before we were anything else, we made sure to leave this little chink, a sort of release valve within our relationship. In the beginning this had meant threesomes, even one or two genuine orgies, mostly at Fire Island Pines and usually brought upon by our other housemate out there, Don Eike, a true "orgy flint" if I ever met one.

Then as Bob and I became professionally more active, that openness was reduced to one Thursday a month, when he'd go his way for the night—usually to a bathhouse—and I'd go my way: to a backroom bar, a sex-club, or sometimes just out to dinner with a friend.

When it became clear that HIV was sexually transmitted, and that we were right at the center of the East Coast nexus of infection, this routine also altered. But we were very much products of the Gay Liberation movement we had joined our friends in bringing about. That, after all, meant freedom, especially sexual freedom. So we agreed, that, okay, we could each see someone else if we really had to, but not bring him home, and we would always play it safe.

The truth is, people very close to us were already dying in numbers, and both of us were certain by then that we, too, were already infected. We were just waiting the day when one of a number of certain "marker" symptoms would appear and with it, the final, fatal diagnosis—because the disease was *always* fatal then. Even so, we would not, could not, fully close the door on other people in our lives.

▲

A DECADE INTO our partnership after returning from a workout at Gold's Gym, Bob told me he had met someone he simply had to get to know better, in all senses of the word—Muscles, a young bodybuilder. I am by nature neither jealous nor possessive, so I told Bob, "Well, I did it. I guess it's your turn. Go for it."

His "other man" relationship lasted many months longer than my own had and because Bob was (everyone agreed) a nice, good, ethical, caring and loving person, and not a ruthless, self-absorbed, well-defended narcissist like I am, he didn't know how to end it, long after the "fantasy" elements had played themselves out. But eventually I no longer heard about this other person, Muscles. So I thought, well, good, it's over. By this point both of us were exceptionally and professionally busy. Bob had gone back to school and gotten a New York State law degree, as well as a job, instantly out of law school. He was now practicing in a small firm near Lincoln Center where his charm and ability meant he would quickly become a partner

I was still writing, but I was also the publisher of the Sea-Horse Press, editor in chief of The Gay Presses of New York, and books editor of New York's gay newspaper, *The Native*. I was also working for several charitable organizations, teaching one night a week at an adult writing school, and also nursing ailing and dying friends. Twenty-four hours were not enough for our days.

We slept most nights either at my place or at Bob's. But some nights one of us was up too late or out of town on business, and soon we were seeing less of each other. So when Bob said he was going to be away most of an upcoming Saturday with Muscles, helping with his bodybuilding contest that weekend, I must have looked surprised. I'd thought that ship had sailed. Well, yes and no. Because it turned out Bob had now become Muscles' "patron."

O-kay.

This happened periodically over the next few months. Then one day, two of our weekends happened to dovetail: a rarity. By virtue of my so-called fame as an author, I had been asked to be one of the judges for the Mr. Fire Island Contest, a bodybuilding event. Independently of that fact, Muscles had entered the contest.

Bob and I had stopped going out to the Pines, partly because we were busy all the time. I was told I would be put up in the Cherry Grove Hotel, a great party palace but not terribly conducive to sleep; in fact, not even conducive to perusing a magazine with a lot of pictures. However Bob and I knew people nearby and so we invited ourselves to their place in relative luxury. And instead, we put the young bodybuilder up at the hotel, in the free room meant for ourselves.

Muscles naturally complained that Bob wasn't being helpful enough, meaning around every moment. But who would be, given our circumstances? At any rate, Muscles was eliminated in the prejudging by the other two judges, both of whom had been Mr. Universe. I felt like the cold cut in a puffy bagel sandwich on that panel. So I didn't have to do any, pardon the pun, heavy lifting, while judging. Bob's pal hadn't expected to win, and he'd placed high enough to make him happy. Minutes after the contest and photo-shoot, our hosts swooped down upon us and hurried us into a speedboat, and across the bay water to an expensive South Shore restaurant. Muscles was left to his own devices including numerous slices of the hotel pizza.

Seven or eight months later, another weekend opened up for me and this time Bob said that his body builder pal had hoped I would join them in prepping and readying him for a "meet." I am a writer, and this was something I knew nothing much about, so I said, "Sure, I'll go." I was thinking I might be able to use this experience in some future story, book, or play. This time, the judging took place on Staten Island which I'd visited maybe twice in my life before. The three of us drove out there and hung out at a friend's empty apartment where we watched Bob's pal pump-up, chow-down, then take water pills to lose excessive water build-up so that his musculature would be better defined or "cut" for the actual judging.

In addition, Muscles also had to have a haircut, a nearly total body shave, multiple applications of creams, tanning lotions, and eventually body-glistening oils. Bob helped out, very hands-on, while I watched. At first I thought this could be compared to getting a prize heifer ready for a state fair, or a thoroughbred horse ready for a race; except for the never-ending string of whining, complaining, multiply spouted anxieties, insecurities, fears, imagined slights, and insults coming from Muscles and aimed at guess who? Bob. This made the day-long exercise seem much more like having to coddle and ready a crazed diva for a five minute aria at the Met Opera.

Naturally Bob had to do most of the work and naturally Bob paid for everything. I suppose this was how he was the "patron." He was earning plenty of dough by that time and anyway we always kept our money separate. For all I cared, he could throw it out of a bus window. And as far as I was concerned, it was having the same effect, anyway.

To my credit, I went along with the entire thing and never once stuck an ice pick into the eye and then brain of Muscles, tempted as I was on numerous occasions. Instead I kept notes, and was even somewhat—not a lot—helpful.

Our little pumped-up baritone placed third and he was happy and after we all ate in a local restaurant and Muscles had two complete steak dinners.

He then slept the night in Bob's den. Exhausted, Bob and I slept at my place.

But something had occurred. I don't know what, maybe it was Bob seeing his humiliation at the hands of Bluto through my eyes. That Sunday, Bob and I were together, and he felt compelled at the dinner we put together to tell me something about the fantasy he had had, and then also a bit about his overbuilt protégé's sad life history: growing up in the slums of Philadelphia; father left mother with three children and no money; for years on end, they never knew if they could pay the rent or had to leave and find another place to live—a litany of woe.

How this could possibly explain why, for example, Muscles could only use a towel or sheet *one time* before it must be discarded to be laundered was never explained. Nor why he changed clothing and even underwear three times a day. No all that was beyond my poor, simple intelligence to comprehend.

But I can be as unjudgmental as the next guy and so I was.

Two more weekends like that one took place in other boroughs and then the final one in Manhattan, which I only attended as a guest at the judging event at night.

Bob looked completely exhausted to me, never a good sign as he tired easily in general. So I abducted him from the last place, deaf to all questions of what would happen to his muscled protégé. I drove us to his condo, where the phone was turned off for the night and morning. I even woke up early and called Bob's law office and told the ladies there that he'd be in after lunch. I watched him sleep which he always did very thoroughly and very sexily.

The next few weeks went by without any mention of the cause of all that exhaustion. Finally when I asked, Bob said he'd instructed his staff at work not to accept any calls from Muscles and he was screening his own calls. I thought, well, that's that. But I misunderstood, never mind underestimated, the power of sheer neediness.

At any rate one weekend while Bob was out of town on business, and to my utter astonishment, I received a phone call from guess who? Mr. Muscles! How he'd gotten my number was a mystery. It was always unlisted. Maybe he'd copied it from Bob's phonebook sometime earlier.

I told him Bob was out of town, confirming what his assistant had told Muscles. No matter, he wanted to meet with me.

I set up a coffee date in a local diner and brought only cash enough for my coffee and a Danish.

Muscles arrived late, sailing in breezily, looking well, and not apparently suffering from the separation.

Not apparently. When all the prefatory chitchat was over, he said to me, and I am not kidding, "I keep wracking my brains wondering how to get rid of you."

Equally cold blooded, I replied, "It's never going to happen. I'm there to the very end. Bob no longer likes the person he is around you. He wants out. For good!"

"Next month I've got a round of body building events leading to a final in…"

"We'll be down in the Caribbean during all that. Bob set it up. We're staying at his partner Lucille's vacation house in the Turks & Caicos Islands. He got the air tickets and all. It's all set. Bob set up the trip and sprang it on me."

This left Muscles musing. I'd ordered separate checks and called for mine and paid it right there on the spot.

He tried once more. "I just don't understand, why. I mean look at me and look at you."

"Let me give you a little tip, sweetheart. The way to a man like Bob's heart is not through his eyes, or his dick or ass, it's through his mind. And let's face it, there I've got you beat several times over. I've got to go. Be well, and please don't call again."

He didn't. Not for a year or so.

During that time, whenever he'd come up as a topic between Bob and me, Muscles had been nicknamed The Child because of Bob's belief in The Child's utter neediness and in his complete inability to get on in life without a lot of help from other people. I called him The Child because I'd seen him carry on like a child whenever he didn't get what he wanted. Bob was relieved however and relaxed. That lasted until his diagnosis for HIV arrived.

I later found out that The Child and Bob met in the waiting room of a doctor's office, where he had helped bring a friend. By then Bob was already obviously ill and The Child wasn't stupid, so that meeting went nowhere fast.

Even so, The Child stuck around and at a close enough distance so that while I didn't hear about him, he was still on the periphery of Bob's life—definitely not even secondary—but somehow there. This is not something I at all understand. When I'm over someone, business, pleasure or friend, it's a good twenty years before they ever see me again and it's only by accident. But hey, I'm a bitch. Bob was good.

▲

I HAD TO be out of town for OutWrite, a gay literary conference, held in Boston, and Bob wasn't feeling well. In the past few months, I'd been watching him, sleeping in a different bed, or on the sofa, but keeping an eye on him. He was the one who insisted I take the three-day trip, and the truth was, I needed the distraction.

How The Child discovered I was gone, I never found out. Did he bribe the doorman of Bob's building? Blow him? Who knew? But The Child was there, trying to get Bob to do something or other for him the very morning that Bob woke up with shooting pains in his chest and back, sure signs of pneumonia.

The Child called me in desperation from Bob's place—Bob

had my hotel number—and left the message. I called back and he was frightened enough by my tone of voice and by Bob's appearance and moans and groans, to spend all day getting Bob into intensive care via the emergency room. Bless him for that. I flew back as soon as I could.

The next five weeks were a nightmare. Bob's mother, Fafner the dragon, showed up. She wanted him out of the hospital and transferred to one of her choice in Boston. No way—the doctors said he was too ill. She wanted this, she wanted that. She was used to manipulating and controlling everyone around her. She'd been doing it for sixty years.

But this time she got nothing of what she asked. Turned out that I held Bob's complete health proxy and medical will. I was the one who had to be contacted, who would have to sign off on any procedure, even if it were an extra aspirin. Even so, she was with him all day, and that was no good at all. She'd been a verbally and physically abusive witch of a mother and the ruin of his early life. It had taken him two decades, and loads of love from other people, to escape her baleful influence.

But of course I put up with her. Bob had never followed my repeated advice to tell his family of his HIV condition, which he'd known for a year, and this woman was clearly in shock and pain. I helped assuage that a little, all the while keeping the facts in front of her. "When he gets over this episode, there will be more and worse ones, probably for the next two years," I told her. After all, that was how the disease had played out time and again, among our friends, in my long and awful experience.

But Bob fooled us. He left much more quickly, and then his mother was nowhere to be found. I was called in to try to mediate by phone with Bob's bereaved mother and Lucille, his bereaved, angry law firm partner who had a notarized will declaring that Bob had to be cremated in the state of New York. There were other things in the will, too, none of them at all happy-making to Fafner the dragon.

The Child showed up, too. Bob had co-signed and co-owned (and probably paid for) the pick-up truck The Child was using daily. The vehicle had to be transferred to his name only now. Naturally this entailed more dealings with Lucille—and with Fafner.

Finally all that messiness was settled. Bob's ashes were hauled to Long Meadow, Massachusetts, not strewn as Bob had requested, but, I was told, to be buried, in line with Jewish tradition. I thought, more likely, they'd be dissolved in a tea for his mother to drink, so she could utterly and finally control his existence.

And I was alone.

By the terms of Bob's will, I was left everything in Bob's apartment. A week after he died, I finally got up the nerve to go there to see what personal effects of his that might entail, expecting to find these items or remembrances causing even more grief and pain.

Instead I found all four rooms, all fifteen hundred square feet of his flat, totally empty, stripped of every single thing that could be carried off, including electrical outlets and of course a lot of my own stuff, which after several years had naturally enough accumulated there.

When I contacted the attorney handling the estate I was told that there was no estate left to make a claim on. His mother had emptied all of his accounts.

So after sixteen years, I got Bob's Bill Robinson linen and rayon jacket made in Hong Kong as an inheritance. While his millionaire mother got all of our things. Naturally at the time, I wondered if Bob knew exactly what would happen after he was dead. Was that why he wanted me to have the jacket? That one thing of his?

I never discovered who had robbed the place: Fafner or The Child. Either were prime candidates. Detectives called in got nowhere.

Frankly, at the time, I didn't much care. I was deeply grieving my soul mate who left me far too soon—it's now half of my lifetime ago. I would soon enter a two-year depression, which severely tested every one of the few remaining friendships I had, a depression that ended only long after I'd left New York for good.

▲

ONCE AGAIN, HOWEVER, before I could get away, The Child located me.

I had spent two-and-a-half years since Bob's death on national book tours, then on one across Western Europe, as well as traveling in the Far East, and then living in Berlin, Germany.

But I'd kept my Manhattan apartment and a pal from Philadelphia stayed there those nights he did not want to commute from New York. I also had the same New York phone number. And somehow, in that brief window of less than a month before I left the East Coast for good, I got a call from The Child.

I was cordial and vaguely interested, as one is interested in the character of a play one saw some time ago and remembers indistinctly.

To my astonishment, he invited me to dinner along with his partner.

They lived in a nice building, with an elevator, in the East Village.

I brought a good bottle of wine.

His partner was maybe ten years older than The Child, blond and fair. He also was a body builder, if not as serious about it, and they lived in a cute, well-appointed flat. They made a good, not at all cuisine-y meal, and we finished the wine and all of us acted like new or semi-good old friends. The Child was surprised that I was leaving the city of my birth, but for me it had become a city of death, so *Ta-Ta! Aufwiedersehn! Ciao!*

I remember thinking how this time the Child seemed to have gotten it right. The older guy clearly adored him, and The Child acted like an adult around him. At least around me, he did. Not whiney and needy. So if The Child was being needy and manipulative and exploitative and greedy—I never for an instant doubted it—he was doing it a lot more subtly than before.

Well, *one* of us had learned something.

I never brought up my burgled estate, and no one else did either.

The Child offered to drive me home. I demurred in lieu of a taxi and he insisted on walking me downstairs.

As we stood as much out of the wind as possible, The Child said, "I'm happy." Adding, "You know that was good advice you gave me in that restaurant."

I almost blurted out in disbelief, "You mean that man loves you for your mind?"

But age and grief had tempered me. So instead I wished him good luck.

I have no idea what happened to either of them. This happened in 1995, and I haven't found either of their names listed in the current online, Tri-state White Pages. Naturally, I suspect the worst.

A Brief History of the Divorce Party
Rob Byrnes

WERE YOU AT The Divorce Party?

No? You really should have been there. It was one of those transitional moments, the type of event everyone would later swear they attended. Even if they weren't present—although most were—false memory would convince them they had witnessed every awkward minute of the evening. They would swear to the feel of the fabric covering the sofa, the specific brand of vodka that was poured, the color of The Other Man's shirt...

But more about The Other Man soon enough. *Too* soon enough. For now, just know that on a chilly Saturday evening in December 1999, dozens of people came to drink and laugh and drink some more while they watched a relationship stagger past the finish line and collapse in its death throes before their very eyes. "I was at The Divorce Party" was their Woodstock, their Stonewall, their Barneys Warehouse Sale.

You should have been there. You would have *loved* it.

No one sets out to host a Divorce Party, of course. But sometimes a Divorce Party is what life hands you. This particular event was *supposed* to be a holiday party, until—one week before scores of people were expected at our Upper West Side duplex to celebrate those holidays—my boyfriend arrived home and announced he was in love with another man.

You know the cliché, "the only surprise was that I was surprised?" Yeah, that.

We'd been a couple for more than ten years—seven long-distance and three in the same apartment—but time and proximity had not brought us closer together. Quite the opposite. With each passing day, it seemed as if bad habits and petty annoyances magnified. My drinking, and his self-righteousness about that. My smoking, and his self-righteousness about that. *His* drinking and smoking, and my self-righteousness about his hypocrisy...

You get the drift. The small incompatibilities one could overlook during those long-distance years, knowing that face-time ended with the weekend, grew larger and more irritating when the relationship became a very real 24/7 thing. And as much as I like to think I'm free of character flaws or vague imperfections, I've been cursed with just enough self-awareness to know my negatives were growing as grating as his. Probably *more* grating. I'm quite unforgiving of myself sometimes.

Still Sam and I—let's call him Sam; all names have been changed to protect the guilty—were a long-term couple, and I assumed we'd grow past those petty annoyances. Or at least get used to them and move on, like one dealt with ragweed allergies (mine), psoriasis (mine), and male-pattern baldness (his). Not ideal, but far from fatal. All human beings in a relationship had to weather the same basic incompatibilities that any two distinct personalities would have. This was a challenge gay men shared with the animals. And with heterosexuals, for that matter. If *they* could do it, I was sure *we* could.

We shared ten years of history, after all. Travel, television shows, jokes, theater, friends, moments of incredible stupidity, passionate nights, so much more...Remembrances no one else shared. Remembrances no one else ever *would* share.

▲

OKAY, SO NOW we know how wrong I was. Many random two- and four-legged couples in the animal kingdom can do that; *we* could not. But we didn't know that when we set the date for our holiday party, and we didn't know that while we invited everyone from close friends to random strangers through the weeks leading up to that fateful day in December, 1999.

Scores of people—some of whom I was barely on a first-name basis with, most of whom were given the date, time, and address on a cocktail napkin collected from one of the half-dozen bars I was frequenting at the time—had been invited to this party. Even as I stormed out of that apartment—my home, or rather, my *former* home—ten minutes after hearing, "I'm in love with another man," never to return as a resident, I focused on all those people I'd invited to a party that...*wouldn't* happen? *Shouldn't* happen?

What was I supposed to do about all those people? There was no way I'd track them all down over the following week. And would it even be my problem anymore? Shouldn't Sam clean up this mess?

I'm not by nature a lightning-fast problem-solver, but I solved my immediate concern—shelter for the following month—by the end of that day. Then I called a few friends to fill them in on the news and get some advice.

The gay men were sympathetic and ambivalent about whether or not the party should go on.

The straight women were sympathetic, but insisted I hold my head high and continue with plans to co-host that damn party. My partner—my ex-partner, that is—would be shamed by my grace. And it wasn't as if Sam would be tacky enough to bring The Other Man, right?

Right. But more on that, too, soon enough.

Oh, and the women told me—each and every one—to take the furniture. Seriously. Four straight women and four uniform and un-solicited opinions: "Take the furniture." Is this a Female Thing?

I didn't take the furniture—first, I had no desire; second, where the hell was I supposed to put an apartment full of furni-ture when I was all but living on the street? But I did agree that the party should go on.

I would hold my head high and be a most charming host.

It would be a breeze.

You know, taking the furniture and setting up camp at the curb would have been easier.

▲

AS I WALKED up the front stoop to the West 89th Street apartment I'd shared until 174 hours earlier before my self-imposed exile, I polished two rules in my head until they gleamed.

Rule One: Hold your head high. You didn't create this fiasco, and you have nothing to apologize for.

Rule Two: Stay cool. Don't let anything get to you.

Both rules fell apart within roughly eight minutes. But you probably saw that coming. Everyone else certainly did.

The fact is this: My temper was a kettle of scalding rage, at any moment just seconds away from a major eruption. Yes, my personality was perforated with flaws, but I didn't deserve this.

I'd just been dumped; no, not just dumped, but dumped and replaced by someone just slightly more than half my age.

I was also suddenly homeless and less-suddenly broke. It was easy to overlook "broke" when I had a home. Now, not so much.

And it was days before my birthday. Days before Christmas. Days before the Y2K New Year's Eve, which promised to be special, if for no other reason that it'd be the only time we'd ever cross into a new millennium.

So when I walked into that apartment one hour before guests were expected and saw that Sam hadn't done a thing to prepare—hadn't picked up, hadn't cleaned, hadn't even showered yet—my Irish temper got a little, well, *Irish*.

Self-awareness aside to the reader: I know I don't do "angry" very well. When I am angry, I'm not Bette Davis drily spitting venom. I'm more like the Incredible Hulk on a very bad day when he's also out of coffee and traffic is backed up. But once the anger dissipates, I'm fine. Mostly.

So after falling apart because Sam was still wandering around in hospital scrubs early on a Saturday evening without even the questionably passable excuse that he was a surgeon, I got over it and got down to business.

We *were* expecting guests after all. And they, no doubt, were expecting us to entertain them.

And those guests did arrive. More people than I'd remembered inviting. The irony is if there hadn't been a break-up the week before, half the people wouldn't have shown. They didn't come because they were unaware of the underlying drama; they came because they wanted to see it play out, live and in-person.

If they wanted entertainment, they got it. It was less cage fighting than tennis, but we still offered our guests a spectator sport.

▲

IT'S NEVER VERY hard to frame oneself as The Victim, especially if you play it right. In a situation like this—dumped for a boy half one's age just before your birthday, the holidays, and the Y2K New Year's Eve, leaving you homeless, impoverished, and kiss-less when the ball would be dropping—it was damn easy. Even with the knowledge that my personal flaws most likely led us to this point, I was determined to play The Victim. I kept my temper in check and my eyes downcast, and sympathy was the only thing that flowed faster than vodka.

As the pace of the party picked up, I held court in the center of the action—meaning, of course, the coffin-sized kitchen—and received a constant audience of friends and acquaintances, half-whispered well-wishes on their lips. Projecting outward calm, I would nod and thank them. Maybe the coffin-sized kitchen was symbolic; this had the feel of a receiving line at a wake.

Meanwhile, Sam stood on the opposite side of the apartment, and I noted with some satisfaction that he was holding briefer conversations with a smaller number of people. No doubt he was making his case—maybe it even worked with a few people—but I wore the bleeding heart of martyrdom, even as the women leaned in to ask when I was going to take that furniture. If you didn't know any better—which, of course, everyone did—you wouldn't think it was *his* apartment, his *furniture*, for that matter, and my status was really no more than a guest that evening.

The party continued for a few hours, the tension at a very low-grade level, until I sensed conversation slowly quieting until the chatter from the living room was muted and awkward.

I looked around the corner from the kitchen and thought, *of course.*

It's not that I didn't expect The Other Man to be invited to The Divorce Party. It was his new boyfriend's apartment, after all, and Sam was more than occasionally deficient in the social graces. I just figured The Other Man would have the good sense to take a pass.

Again, I was wrong.

I suspect he came to regret it, but it really wasn't my problem. Jerry—the kid I was shoved aside for—would spend the next few hours standing in one corner, mostly ignored by the other guests, while I held court in that tiny kitchen and drank too much.

If Jerry noticed my glares, he pretended he didn't. But I can't imagine it was possible he missed them. If so, I was doing it wrong.

⚜

AFTER THE DIVORCE Party, I had little to do with Sam, and even less with Jerry. With the infrequent exception of stopping by my former residence on West 89th Street to collect mail or items left behind in my rushed exit, my new life quickly grew separate from my old life. By February, I'd even found a more or less stable place to live and was actively working to rebuild my life. I was even dating again, although…well, those are stories for another anthology.

The important thing was that I was recovering. It wasn't the same, and it wasn't always good, but it was progress. The fear and anger and queasy stomach that had plagued me for months were slowly easing. Sometimes whole hours would pass when I wouldn't think of the great wrong, the horrible indignities, that had befallen me and *probably destroyed my life forever!*

I'd just about settled into the new routine when the recent past began to return.

It began one day when a friend—since I'm trying to keep real names out of this, let's just call him Carl—called to see if I needed a ride to that evening's dinner party at the home of Rick and Paul.

To which I said, "Uh, *what* dinner party?"

To which Carl said, "Oops."

You think you know people. You spend years building a shared history full of inside jokes and life experiences, to the point when if someone starts a sentence with "Remember that time…?" you're off and running and the conversation flows seamlessly. You assume the friendships you've built together mean your lives are inseparable.

But when you're wrong, you're wrong.

Okay, despite my self-importance I recognize that I shouldn't expect to be invited to every dinner party. There are only so many seats at any given table. Although Rick and Paul had *always* invited me to past dinner parties, there was no reason to expect I'd be a permanent fixture. Sure, I'd been on *every* guest list in the past, but that was no guarantee I'd be invited forever. And I contented myself with that thought as I drank myself to sleep and wondered why I'd been axed from the guest list and how friends could possibly do that to me when I was so vulnerable and how I'd get revenge one day…

No doubt you're ahead of me here, because—sure

enough—the next day I learned that Rick and Paul had replaced me at their table with Sam. *And* Jerry.

The fact that my ex only knew my friends of more than a decade because of our past relationship was irrelevant. Absolutely not a factor. I had been tossed aside, and my place had been filled. I had become...disposable.

It was the first time that had happened in the wake of The Divorce Party—or maybe it was the first time I'd been made aware of it—but not the last. As the months unfolded, I found myself bumped in favor of the new fun couple more than a few times. Oh, if it were a competition I could still fairly claim I was far in the lead, and by quite a large margin, but that wasn't the problem.

The problem was that The Other Man was becoming a semi-regular presence in the lives of my friends. And every point he had on the board was one point too many.

I wasn't a fan of that concept. My victory over The Other Man was supposed to be a shutout, if not a perfect game.

▲

IN THE AFTERMATH of The Divorce Party, when I spent hours glaring at him, I almost never saw Jerry. Everyone exercised enough common sense to keep us at such a distance that he might as well have been living in Montana. I certainly knew where he'd been—I never asked, but people liked to tell—and I suspect he knew whenever my path crossed Sam's. But I saw him so infrequently I barely remembered what he looked like on those very rare occasions we ended up in the same room. I'd just assume the ugliest, fattest, most awkward, poorly dressed man in the room had to be him.

A notable exception was a holiday party hosted by Rick and Paul a few years after The Divorce Party. They'd apparently assumed that enough time had passed and everyone could be mature and adult about the situation, and, for the most part, they were right. When I heard that all the players would be in the same house, I knew I could be mature and adult. If ugly, fat, awkward, poorly dressed Jerry stayed the hell out of my way. Outside the house would have been a good place for him. Maybe down the hill in the dog run.

He stayed in the kitchen for most of the night. It wasn't the dog run, but it was all right because it wasn't near me. In fact, he was in the kitchen—hiding, I'd decided, with no evidence to back me up—while several of us, including Sam, sat in front of the fireplace toward the end of the evening, draining our twenty-third bottle of wine. The conversation skipped over old, familiar territory, centered on those shared jokes formed over years and years, which no mere *newcomer* could hope to fully understand. Even now it would be pointless for me to try to fill you in on what, exactly, made things like "the blue decanter," "pink drinks," and "the burning pizza box" pants-wettingly funny after all those years. You would have had to be there, and even then it'd only be funny if you'd been drinking. A lot.

After a while, Sam began to nod off in front of the fire. Out of the corner of my eye, I spotted Jerry in a doorway, poised to wake him up and probably take him home.

So I acted quickly and made my move.

It wasn't what you think. I knew that thing between us had ended years earlier, and I'd moved on. But Jerry—who'd taken my place in Sam's bed—needed to be put in his *own* place. After a night filled with verbal shortcuts and in-jokes that defined our inner circle—a circle in which I was in the center and mostly included Sam but definitely *not* his boyfriend—I realized I had one ace in the hole.

I couldn't and didn't want to rekindle my old relationship, but I could and did want to remind The Other Man that I had standing. He might be the newer, shinier, much younger object, but I'd been there earlier and for a lot more history.

So I leaned over Sam, guided him gently into a sitting posi-tion, and spoke softly, coaxing him awake and asking if he wanted water or coffee. The other old-timers in the room pretended nothing was other than normal; I figured they would. It really *had been* normal for us in the not too distant past.

Jerry, well…he wasn't glaring—he wouldn't dare—and he certainly wasn't jealous, but he seemed acutely, maybe abruptly, aware that he was the outsider.

And always would be.

Which was the adult, mature point I had intended to make. Hey, the kid got off without getting a wedgie, so give me a little credit.

In a strange way, that little stunt made me feel better about myself. I was an insider, even if I was dropped from the occasional invitation list to make room for those other men. I'd been around and paid my dues, and I had something with all those people—something even with Sam—that Jerry would never have in quite the same way.

I had history. I had standing.

He had his own status: The Home-wrecker. The Other Man.

Was I fair? Hell, no. But when you're the one who was kicked to the curb, fairness is a luxury. And it was always easier taking out my residual anger on Jerry. We had no history.

▲

THINGS CHANGE.

Years earlier, I'd been all but homeless, very broke, and had no one to kiss on the Y2K New Year's Eve. But life got better, and fairly quickly. My employment situation improved, and with it my financial security. I had my own apartment, and eventually found love again. I got published, and what I thought would be an unrealized dream became reality.

More time passed, and as my career and new relationship continued to flourish, my living situation went from passable to nice to enviable. More importantly, when I was entering middle age at the time of The Divorce Party, I'd become far too dependent on other people. Now I was totally independent.

Somehow, and often despite myself, I'd managed to emerge on the other side as a grown-up.

▲

SAM AND JERRY didn't make it. My presence on the periphery of their lives had nothing to do with that, of course, and by the time I heard the news I was strangely unaffected. All that did was allow me to start rebuilding a relationship with my former partner; a relationship that was strictly platonic but could never have gelled until The Other Man was no longer part of his life. I may be forgiving, but I'm not a masochist.

In time, he moved on again. Met someone. Fell in love. Moved in with him. Everyone became friends. I know my problem with Jerry wasn't really *with Jerry*, but—when he was gone—it became much easier to move forward.

One day, more than a dozen years after The Divorce Party and not too long ago, I ran into Sam at a bar. He was distraught but didn't want to tell me what happened, despite the reconciliation we'd gone through.

Then it came out. He'd just learned that his post-Jerry boyfriend had been having an affair. His own relationship had been kayoed by...*another* other man.

Of course he didn't want to tell me. He was afraid I'd gloat and remind him that what goes around comes around.

I didn't. I wouldn't. Maybe ten years earlier, but not today. Time has a way of healing us.

All I could do was embrace Sam and promise I'd be there for him. In a sense, he was there for me, too, because over the ensuing months, as we dissected his latest failed relationship, we had the opportunity to discuss what had happened between us all those years earlier.

It was a conversation we'd both avoided for more than a decade. I felt it would be pointless, since I thought I already knew how we'd come unraveled. Remember: I was self-aware enough to see my character flaws and give them much of the blame. Even as I played the victim, I knew that our break-up had not occurred in a vacuum.

But no. My character flaws were a factor, but not the deciding factor. What drove him to seek The Other Man had less to do with my bad habits, and more to do with his feelings of being trapped. When we split up, Sam was thirty-six years old, and he saw every day of the rest of his life unfolding exactly like the one he'd lived the day before. Same partner, same apartment, same friends telling those same inside jokes. When he broke up with me, it was more a desperate gasp for air than anything personal.

In other words, it was Sam, not me. After twelve years of kicking myself for screwing everything up, I was at least granted the knowledge that I had less to do with the circumstances than I'd thought. It was cold comfort, but it was there.

In the meantime, he was still living with his own now-ex, waiting for him to leave their shared apartment or for the lease to run out, whichever came first. I laughed when I reminded him how I'd stormed out, saving us both from that drama.

"You did," he agreed. After a pause, he said, "And you want to hear something weird? My female friends keep telling me I should make sure I take all the furniture."

Some things *don't* change...

He had the good sense this time not to host a Divorce Party.

And he's keeping the furniture.

The Contributors

PERRY BRASS IS a novelist, playwright, and activist who has published sixteen books. He co-edited the world's first gay liberation newspaper, *Come Out*, published by the Gay Liberation Front of New York. A few years later, with two friends, he founded the Gay Men's Health Project Clinic, the first clinic for gay men on the East Coast, still operating today. Brass's writing often deals with an intersection of sexuality, spirituality, and personal politics stemming directly from his association with the radical politics of the late 1960's and early 1970's. Currently a coordinator of the Rainbow Book Fair, the largest LGBT book fair in the U.S, he is a six-time finalist for the Lambda Literary Award. His latest book is *King of Angels*, a gay, Southern Jewish coming-of-age novel set in Savannah, GA, in 1963, the year of JFK's assassination. He can be reached through his website at perrybrass.com.

AUSTIN BUNN IS a writer and performer. His fiction and non-fiction have appeared in *The Atlantic, New York Times Magazine, The Advocate, The Best American Science and Nature Writing, The Pushcart Prize*, and elsewhere. His plays have been performed and developed at the Actors' Theatre of Louisville, The New Harmony Project, Playwrights Theatre of NJ, Playwrights' Center, The Lark, Third Coast's *Re:Sound* radio program and on Australian radio. He wrote the screenplay, *Kill Your Darlings*, about Allen Ginsberg and the origins of the Beat Generation, with the director John Krokidas, which premiered at Sundance 2013. He teaches at Cornell University. A version of "Husbands" first appeared in *The Advocate*, August 12, 2008.

ROB BYRNES IS the author of six highly praised novels, including the Lambda Literary Award-winning comic romance, *When the Stars Come Out*, and the Grant Lambert-Chase LaMarca crime caper series—and a number of short stories. Born and raised in Rochester, NY, he moved to Manhattan in the late 90's to strengthen his relationship and make his fortune. Things didn't quite go as planned, but it got better. By day, he now has a surprisingly responsible job; at night, he returns home to "Manhattan-adjacent" West New York, N.J., where he lives with his partner, Brady Allen. His hobbies include drinking, claiming he'll never write again, procrastinating, and drinking. Visit him at robbyrnes.net.

MARK CANAVERA IS a writer, humanitarian aid worker, and activist who works primarily in West Africa. His humanitarian efforts focus on youth empowerment and child and family welfare in settings impacted by conflict such as former child soldier reintegration in northern Uganda, small arms control in Senegal, girls' education promotion in Burkina Faso, and child welfare system reform in Côte d'Ivoire and Niger. Mark was a founding editor of the *Harvard Africa Policy Journal* and served on the editorial staff of the *Harvard Journal of African American Public Policy*. He writes features and op-ed pieces on African affairs and blogs at The *Huffington Post*. Mark received Harvard University's prestigious 2008 Robert F. Kennedy Award for Public Service. He won the 1999 L.D. Johnson Award for Creative Writing/Film Review at Furman University, and the 1996 Best Feature Story Award from the South Carolina Press Association.

R.W. CLINGER is a resident of Pittsburgh. He has a degree in English from Point Park University of Pittsburgh. His writing entails gay human studies. His work includes the novels *Nebraska Close, Just a Boy, Skin Tour, Skin Artist, Soft on the Eyes, Pool Boy,* and *The Last Pile of Leaves.* Rob has published many stories with Starbooks Press as well as *The Weekender,* a novella with Dreamspinner Press. His gay mystery, *Cutie Pie Must Die,* is published with Bold Stroke Books. *The Boyfriend Season,* his first book of short stories, is published with JMS Books, as well as the novella *The Author's Assistant.* His other novellas include *Frat Brats, Panama Dan, Spoil Me So, The Shower Police,* and *Splash Boys.* For three years he has held the position of managing editor for the literary magazine, *The Writer's Post Journal.* Rob is currently at work on a gay cowboy trilogy set in Oklahoma, which will be published in 2014. He is also at work on his third gay mystery, *Mechanics, Men and Murder.* For more information, visit rwclinger.com or e-mail him at kenitoricorico@verizon.net.

LEWIS DESIMONE IS the author of *The Heart's History,* cited by both Band of Thebes and the Rainbow Awards as one of the best LGBT books of 2012. His first novel, *Chemistry,* was published in 2006. Lewis's work has also appeared in *Chelsea Station, Christopher Street, James White Review, Harrington Gay Men's Fiction Quarterly,* and the anthologies *Dirty Diner, Second Person Queer: Who You Are (So Far), The Mammoth Book of Threesomes and Moresomes, Charmed Lives: Gay Spirit in Storytelling, Best Gay Love Stories:*

Summer Flings, I Like It Like That: True Tales of Gay Male Desire, and *My Diva: 65 Gay Men on the Women Who Inspire Them*. His contribution to the latter was highlighted on Salon and reprinted in *Ganymede* and *Best Gay Stories 2010*. He blogs regularly at SexAndTheSissy.wordpress.com and can be reached through his Web site, lewisdesimone.com. He lives in San Francisco, where he is working on his next novel.

PAUL ALAN FAHEY, Ed.D, lives on the Central California Coast. He created and edited *Mindprints*, an international literary journal for writers and artists with disabilities, at Allan Hancock College in Santa Maria, California. During his tenure, *Mindprints* made *Writers Digest*'s "Top 30 Short Story Markets" list for two consecutive years. His writing has appeared in *Byline, Palo Alto Review, Long Story Short, African American Review, The MacGuffin, Thema, Gertrude, Kaleidoscope, The Feathered Flounder*, and in several other literary journals and anthologies. Paul's first novella, *The View From 16 Podwale Street*, published by JMS Books, won a 2012 Rainbow Award. He is a seven-time winner of the "Lillian Dean Writing Award" for short stories and nonfiction at the California Central Coast Writer's Conference. Paul lives on the Nipomo mesa with his partner, Robert Franks, and a gaggle of shelties. A version of "Where Are You Going To?" first appeared in *paperplates*, 2002. Visit him at paulalanfahey.com.

WES HARTLEY IS an ambidextrous multi-tasker with a penchant for up-and-comers. He's been accused of being a polymath and of being too big for his britches. He is currently employed as a bullion trader—he always goes for the gold—and he's a freelance speculator in the global fine art market. Wes is an avid collector of paintings and he's written several books. He is seriously laid back and easygoing. He is a vegan tree-hugger struggling to downsize his embarrassingly sacrilegious carbon footprint and an unrepentant willing victim of splendid youths and their masculine pursuits. Wes works tirelessly in his community on behalf of LGBT youth, and he volunteers as an intervener speaking in their language to high schoolers on the ongoing Anti-Bullying Initiative. Wes lives in Vancouver, Canada.

WILLIAM HENDERSON HAS written for and been published in newspapers, magazines, and journals around the world, including *The Huffington Post, Thought Catalog, Life By Me*, and he reviews books for the *Heavy Feather Review*. He lives in Boston, where he works as a freelance editor and content producer; cares for his two children, Avery and Aurora; and devours comic books, memoirs, and bestsellers. He is a frequent contributor to the *Pure Slush* anthology imprint; the magazine, *Mental Shoes*; blogs at hendersonhouseofcards.com; and frequently tweets about life, love, parenting, writing, and sex @Avesdad.

ALLEN MACK HAS spent most of his life working as a flight attendant for an international airline, having visited some seventy countries on all continents over a period of years. His greatest loves have always been reading, writing, and travel—all of which he has managed to enjoy singly or simultaneously when time permitted. He grew up in New York City writing short stories first, then poetry, plays, and a novel. Allen claims that his writing is the result of expanding on actual experiences, the pleasure he feels when his imagination comes into play, the insight he tries for when he hears of others' lives, whether happy or dramatic or even mundane. New people are as new worlds, many facets and ages to be explored. The world has introduced Allen to exotic venues, peopled with equally rare personalities, a world with oh-so-many different sizes and shapes, cultures and beliefs.

JEFF MANN'S BOOKS include three collections of poetry, *Bones Washed with Wine, On the Tongue*, and *Ash: Poems from Norse Mythology*; two books of personal essays, *Edge: Travels of an Appalachian Leather Bear* and *Binding the God: Ursine Essays from the Mountain South*; two novellas, *Devoured*, included in *Masters of Midnight: Erotic Tales of the Vampire* and *Camp Allegheny*, included in *History's Passion: Stories of Sex Before Stonewall*; two novels, *Fog: A Novel of Desire* and *Reprisal*, winner of the Pauline Réage Novel Award, and *Purgatory: A Novel of the Civil War*, winner of a Rainbow Award; a collection of poetry and memoir, *Loving Mountains, Loving Men*; and two volumes of short fiction, *Desire and Devour: Stories of Blood and Sweat* and *A History of Barbed Wire*, winner of a Lambda Literary Award. He teaches creative writing at Virginia Tech in Blacksburg, Virginia.

TOM MENDICINO IS a graduate of the University of Pennsylvania and the University of North Carolina School of Law whose debut novel, *Probation*, was named a 2011 American Library Association Stonewall Award Honor Book and was a Lambda Literary Award finalist. His novella, "Away in a Manger," appeared in the Kensington collection, *Remembering Christmas*, and his short fiction has appeared in numerous anthologies. *Hello, Mary Lou*, the first book of the trilogy *KC, at Bat*, will be published by Kensington in June 2013.

▲

ERIK ORRANTIA WAS born and raised in the San Francisco Bay Area. He has lived in Tijuana since 1998, during which time he has traveled extensively throughout Mexico and has become fluent in Spanish. Teacher by day, writer by night, Erik's first published book, *Normal Miguel* was awarded the 2011 Lambda Literary Award for best gay romance. Erik has written a suspense novel, *The Equinox Convergence*, a third work, *Taxi Rojo*, which deals with life and times in Tijuana, and *Day of the Dead— A Romance*.

FELICE PICANO IS the author of two dozen books of poetry, fiction, memoir, and non-fiction. His work has been translated into fifteen languages including Chinese, Hebrew, and Slovenian, and several titles were national and international bestsellers. His first novel was a PEN/Hemingway Award finalist. At the 2004 Tennessee Williams Festival, Felice won the Violet Quill Life Achievement Award. *The New York Times* listed *Art & Sex in Greenwich Village* as one of 100 Best Books of 2007. In 2009, The Lambda Literary Foundation presented him with their Lifetime Achievement/Pioneer Award. Recent publications include an anthology of LGBT Latino-American fiction titled *Ambientes: New Queer Latino Writing*, a memoir, *True Stories: Portraits From My Past*, as well as short stories collected in *Contemporary Gay Romances* and *Twelve O'Clock Tales*. In 2013, Picano's play *The Bombay Trunk*, will be produced in Peterborough, Canada, and two of Felice's short novels will be published as *20th Century Unlimited*.

DAVID PRATT, WRITER, director, and performer, has published short fiction in *Christopher Street*, *The James White Review*, *Blithe House Quarterly*, *Harrington Gay Men's Fiction Quarterly*, *Velvet Ma-*

fia, and in the anthologies *Men Seeking Men*, *His3*, *Fresh Men 2*, and *The Dirty Diner*. He has directed and performed his own work for the theater, including appearances in New York City at the Cornelia Street Café, Dixon Place, HERE Arts Center, the Flea Theater, and the Eighth Annual New York International Fringe Festival. His first published novel, *Bob the Book*, received the 2011 Lambda Literary Award for Gay Debut Fiction. His short story collection, *My Movie*, is out from Chelsea Station Editions. It includes his first published work, "The Addict," referred to in his essay.

GLEN RETIEF'S MEMOIR about growing up white and gay in apartheid South Africa, *The Jack Bank*, won a 2011 Lambda Literary Award and was selected as an Africa Book Club Book of the Year. His writing has appeared in numerous journals here and abroad, including *Virginia Quarterly Review*, *The Greensboro Review*, *The James White Review*, *The Massachusetts Review*, and the flagship South African journal *New Contrast*. Glen has published newspaper articles and op-ed pieces in *The St. Petersburg Times*, *The Pittsburgh Post-Gazette*, and *The Harrisburg Patriot-News*. He has held numerous fellowships and awards including a James Michener Writing Fellowship and a Florida State University Fellowship—the university's most prestigious award for graduate students. His essay, "Keeping Sodom Out of the Laager," appeared in *Defiant Desire*, the first-ever anthology of South African lesbian and gay writing. He teaches creative nonfiction at Susquehanna University.

JEFFREY RICKER'S FIRST novel, *Detours*, was published in 2011 by Bold Strokes Books. His writing has appeared in the anthologies *Paws and Reflect, Fool for Love: New Gay Fiction, Blood Sacraments, Men of the Mean Streets, Speaking Out, Riding the Rails*, and others. He is currently finishing his second novel and pursuing an MFA in creative writing at the University of British Columbia. When class is out, he lives in St. Louis with his partner, Michael, and two dogs. Follow his blog at jeffreyricker.wordpress.com.

RODNEY ROSS IS the author of *The Cool Part of His Pillow*, his debut novel from Dreamspinner Press. Fiction, however, is not alien to Ross. He is a former advertising creative director, so he's accustomed to molding mountains out of molehills, treating facts as wholly malleable, and, bluntly put, making shit up. Past achievements include multiple ADDY Awards and an optioned screenplay and play (both currently unproduced). Other screenplays earned Honorable Mentions or runners-up citations in the Monterey County Film Commission, FADE-IN and the LGBT One-In-Ten Screenwriting Competitions. Most recently, he won the "Most Creative" citation in the 2012 Key West Mystery Fest writing competition. He is also a producer of the upcoming documentary, *The Little Firemen*. He lives in Key West, Florida, where he carefully listens to the island's literary ghosts as he works on his next novel.

JASON SCHNEIDERMAN, ESSAYIST and poet, is the author of *Sublimation Point* and *Striking Surface*. His poetry and essays have appeared in numerous journals and anthologies, including *American Poetry Review, The Best American Poetry, Poetry London, Grand Street, The Penguin Book of the Sonnet, Story Quarterly*, and *Tin House*. Author Michael Montlack featured Jason's essay about Liza Minnelli in his book, *My Diva: 65 Gay Men on the Women Who Inspire Them*. Jason has received fellowships from Yaddo, The Fine Arts Work Center, and The Bread Loaf Writers' Conference. He won the

2009 Richard Snyder Prize from Ashland Poetry Press. He was also the recipient of The Emily Dickinson Award from the Poetry Society of America in 2004. Jason directs the Writing Center at the Borough of Manhattan Community College.

PHILIP DEAN WALKER'S fiction has previously appeared in *Big Lucks, Collective Fallout, Obsession Lit Mag,* and *Jonathan.* He holds a B.A. in American Literature from Middlebury College and is an M.F.A. candidate at American University in Creative Writing. He resides in Washington, D.C.

CHUCK WILLMAN IS a self-taught writer published with JMS Books. His poetry has appeared in *A&U* magazine; *A&U: The 20th Anniversary Anthology* (Black Lawrence Press); *Tricks, Johns, Marks, and Chickenhawks: Professionals Writing on Life, Love, Money, and Sex* (Soft Skull Press); *ppigpenn* (an online journal); *Assaracus: A Journal of Gay Poetry, Nurturing Paws* (Whispering Angel Books), and *Christopher Street* magazine. His erotica has been published in the anthology, *Cruising,* and is forthcoming in *Big Man on Campus* (Cleis Press). Other stories have appeared in *FirstHand, Manscape,* and *Guys* magazines under the pseudonym Ethan Cox. He has published essays on sex and HIV/AIDS, and he writes a column on AIDS & Aging for *A&U.* Chuck lives with his partner of twenty-five years in the Las Vegas area. Contact the writer via e-mail at pozchuck@live.com.

ACKNOWLEDGEMENTS

THIS ANTHOLOGY CAME about mainly through my good fortune. It's one of those stories you hear about: X happened first, then Y, and lastly Z as each chance element fell neatly into place. In my case, it all started with Z when I met the wonderful Victoria Zackheim, writer, essayist, anthologist, playwright, and editor. Without Victoria's guidance, constant support, motherly advice, and great humor, this book would not have happened the way it did. At least for me. Specifically, if I hadn't attended the 2010 California Central Coast Writers' Conference, taken Victoria's workshop on writing and editing personal essays and spoken with her the following day at the San Luis Obispo Author Book Fest, well…you get the idea. So first and foremost I want to thank Victoria for having faith in me, for believing I could carry the project off and be trusted with editing the companion to her wonderful and wildly successful anthology, *The Other Woman.*

I am enormously grateful to my agent, Jill Marsal of the Marsal/Lyon Literary Agency, who shepherded me through the world of publishing—something I knew very little about. If Victoria was my mentor, Jill was my guardian angel.

I also owe a great deal of gratitude to the amazing writers I've worked with during the book's journey from two proposals to print. I especially want to acknowledge those gifted writers, playwrights, and poets attached to the first version including

Guillermo Reyes, Raymond Luczak, Bob Smith, and Timothy Liu among others, as well as the kindness and generosity of Mart Crowley, Don Bachardy, and Edmund White who offered me their work for publication. I indeed had the best of luck.

When the book finally crystallized as a collection of personal essays, my good luck struck gold again, and I couldn't have been more thrilled with the writers whose work appears in this volume. They immediately and wholeheartedly committed to this project and, in the process, courageously bared their souls. I am in great debt to each and every one of them and in awe of their down to the bones honesty, courage and writing brilliance.

I wish to express my gratitude to my publisher, JM Snyder, for believing in our book and for her publishing savvy and professionalism; to my Night Writer support group—you know who you are—and writer pals, Anne R. Allen and Judy the Guarnera, and to so many others for their referrals, encouragement, advice, and editing expertise; and to my partner, Robert Franks, and dear friend, Roger Paris, who were my lifelines every step of the way.

I'm also grateful to Tony Valenzuela and William Johnson at Lambda Literary, Stephen Hemrick of *The Gay and Lesbian Review*, the California Central Coast Gay and Lesbian Alliance (GALA), and editor and writer, Timothy J. Lambert, who all helped to get the word out about the anthology, as well as to the terrific writers, editors, actors, poets, playwrights, and book publishers I met along the way. What an amazing ride this has been. I thank you all.